The Grants Coaching Handbook

The Grants Coaching Handbook

Successful Techniques for Creating and Conducting Grants Coaching Programs

David G. Bauer

ROWMAN & LITTLEFIELD
Lanham • Boulder • New York • London

Published by Rowman & Littlefield
A wholly owned subsidiary of The Rowman & Littlefield Publishing Group, Inc.
4501 Forbes Boulevard, Suite 200, Lanham, Maryland 20706
www.rowman.com

Unit A, Whitacre Mews, 26-34 Stannary Street, London SE11 4AB

Copyright © 2017 by David G. Bauer

All rights reserved. No part of this book may be reproduced in any form or by any electronic or mechanical means, including information storage and retrieval systems, without written permission from the publisher, except by a reviewer who may quote passages in a review.

British Library Cataloguing in Publication Information Available

Library of Congress Cataloging-in-Publication Data Available

ISBN: 978-1-4758-1012-7 (cloth : alk. paper)
ISBN: 978-1-4758-3565-6 (pbk. : alk. paper)
ISBN: 978-1-4758-1013-4 (electronic)

♾️™ The paper used in this publication meets the minimum requirements of American National Standard for Information Sciences—Permanence of Paper for Printed Library Materials, ANSI/NISO Z39.48-1992.

Printed in the United States of America

Contents

List of Exhibits	vii
Preface	ix
Introduction	1
PART I: THE GRANTS COACHING PROGRAM	**5**
1 Goals, Objectives, and Benefits	7
2 Proactive Grant Seeking: The Foundation for an Effective Grants Coaching Program	9
3 Target Population	13
4 Program Outlines, Participant Incentives, Requirements/Benchmarks	17
5 Educational Components	33
6 Estimating the Costs Associated with Your Unique Grants Coaching Program	39
PART II: THE GRANTS COACH	**47**
7 Grants Coaching Basics	49
8 The Role of the Grants Coach	53
9 Helping Coachees Develop Their Career Grants/Research Plans	63
10 Getting Coachees to Focus on the Problem and Measure the Gap	71
11 Assisting Coachees in Developing Advocacy Plans, Consortia, and Teams	73
12 Encouraging Coachees to Develop and Maintain Research/Grant Profiles	79

13	Showing Coachees How to Analyze Federal Grantors to Find the Best Match for Their Research/Projects	85
14	Assisting Coachees in Contacting Federal Program Officers	93
15	Guiding Coachees through the Federal Proposal Development Process	99
16	The Coach's Role in Improving Federal Proposals	103
17	Role of the Coach in the Proposal Submission and Follow-Up Process	113
18	Guiding Coachees through the Foundation/Corporate and Private Proposal Development Process	117
19	Integrating the Institution's/Organization's Grants Administration Staff into Your Grants Coaching Program	125
20	Evaluating and Improving Your Grants Coaching Program	133
	Index	137
	About the Author	139

Exhibits

4.1	Sample Grants Coaching Program Outline: Research Development Award Program	19
4.2	Sample Public Relations/Marketing Piece	21
4.3	Sample Invitation to Participate in a Grants Coaching Program	22
4.4	Sample Grants Coaching Program Outline and Call for Applications: CRADLE Initiative	23
4.5	Sample Grants Program Application	25
4.6	Sample Forty-Five-Minute Sign-Up Sheet	26
4.7	Sample Sixty-Minute Sign-Up Sheet	26
4.8	Sample Grants Coaching Program Agreement	27
4.9	Sample Invitation to Graduation Luncheon	28
4.10	Sample Certificate of Completion	29
4.11	Sample Grants Coaching Program: Research Development Program	29
4.12	Sample Grants Coaching Program Outline: Grants Acquisition Program	30
5.1	Seminar Outline: How to Find—And Win—Government Grants	34
5.2	Seminar Outline: How to Find—And Win—Foundation and Corporate Grants	35
5.3	Seminar Outline: Keys to Increasing Collaboration and Effective Team Building	36
5.4	Seminar Outline: Improving Grant Proposals through Quality Circles	37
6.1	Developing Your Grants Coaching Program and Estimating Costs	40
8.1	Coach's Evaluation of Video-Recorded Session	61
8.2	Coachee's Evaluation/Feedback Form	62
9.1	Your Personal Grants Plan	64
9.2	Sample Personal Grants Plan	68
11.1	Cost–Benefit Analysis Worksheet for Projects/Programs	74
11.2	Cost–Benefit Analysis Worksheet for Research Protocols/Approaches	75
11.3	Skills Required to Win Grants	77
12.1	Redefinition/Key Search Terms Worksheet	80

12.2	Corporate Redefinition Worksheet	82
13.1	Federal Grants Research Form	86
13.2	Program and Past Recipient Analysis Worksheet	88
13.3	Sample E-mail to a Past Grantee Requesting a Copy of His/Her Successful Proposal	89
13.4	Tailoring Worksheet	90
14.1	Possible Questions to Ask a Federal Program Officer	95
14.2	Funding Source Staff Profile	96
14.3	Public Funding Source Contact Summary Sheet	96
14.4	Tailoring Worksheet	97
15.1	Uniqueness Worksheet	100
16.1	Sample Letter/E-mail Inviting an Individual to Participate in a Grants Quality Circle	105
16.2	Federal/State Grants Quality Circle Worksheet	106
16.3	Conducting a Quality Circle Review/Roles	107
16.4	Using Quality Circles to Improve Proposals	109
18.1	Nonprofit Marketplace Quiz	119
19.1	Worksheet on How to Include Administrators Key to Government Proposal Preparation and Submittal	128
19.2	Worksheet on How to Include Administrators Key to Private Proposal Preparation and Submittal	129
19.3	Sample E-mail Inviting Government Grants Administrator to Take Part in Your Seminar	130
19.4	Sample E-mail Inviting Private Grants Administrator (Development Director) to Take Part in Your Seminar	131
20.1	Sample Seminar Evaluation Form	135
20.2	Winning Grant-Seeking Strategy Checklist	136

Preface

Part I of this book provides college, university, and other nonprofit administrators with the basis to assess the appropriateness of using a grants coaching program to improve their organization's grants success. It outlines program components, provides an estimate of the cost/benefits of a grants coaching program, and helps the administrator determine if and when his or her program can utilize an in-house grants coach, an external consultant/grants coach, or both. The book should be thought of as primer for developing grants coaching programs for those administrators who wish to provide this experience to selected faculty and staff.

Part II of this book focuses on the grants coach. It provides those interested in becoming a grants coach with a series of developmental activities designed to facilitate the process of helping others secure funding for projects, programs, and research. It is not designed to be the ultimate guide to grants coaching. But it should lead the prospective grants coach in the right direction and serve as a field guide to those who are currently involved in grants coaching and wish to improve or augment their existing skills.

As you embark on your grants coaching journey, I suggest you begin by reading *The "How To" Grants Manual* (order online at https://rowman.com). This manual (the most recent edition of which was published in 2015) provides the basics on how to find and win federal, foundation, and corporate grants and details the proactive grant-seeking system I refer to throughout this book. It is an excellent reference material for the administrator considering the implementation of a grants coaching program at his or her organization/institution and the consultant looking at becoming a grants coach or refining his or her skills in the area.

In addition, the exhibits from *The "How To" Grants Manual* that are referred to in this publication can be downloaded from the manual for the instructor's and program participants' use. To gain access to these downloads, e-mail textbooks@rowman.com requesting that the supplementary materials for *The "How To" Grants Manual*, eighth edition (ISBN 978-1-4758-1010-3), be sent to you at your e-mail address.

The creation of this book has been a tall order. However, I had collaborators and colleagues who encouraged and supported me by providing ideas on what to include.

Special thanks to the people I have worked with who have been instrumental in the support and development of my grants coaching programs at the University of Alabama, Wake Forest University, University of North Carolina Greensboro, Western Michigan University, Marquette University, and the State University of New York at Cortland. Based on their suggestions and my own experiences and expertise in the grants coaching field, I am hopeful that the reader will be able to put this book's content into use to help others achieve grants success and understand how grants success can move them where they want to be.

Introduction

The first question that should come to mind when you pick this book up is "What is grants coaching?" To answer this question, one must understand what is meant by the words "grant" and "coaching."

A grant refers to a proposal submitted to a funding source (grantor) that culminates in the exchange of money or other form of support (i.e., equipment, laboratory access, loaned personnel, and so on). The source of the grant is usually a government agency, a private foundation, or a corporate entity. On rare occasions the grantor or funding source is an individual who does not have a private foundation. However, these exchanges are most commonly defined as a gift.

Since most grants are governed by federal and state requirements (public grants) or regulated by Internal Revenue Service rules (private grants), the majority of the $550 billion granted each year in the United States is awarded to grantees that are 501(c)3 tax exempt organizations. Profit-making corporations are eligible for some grants and do get a small portion of the grants marketplace through programs like Small Business Innovation Research. While individuals are technically eligible to apply for and receive some federal grants, they rarely appear on grantee lists. Support for individuals from federal funds is usually considered a benefit and not a grant.

Now that you understand what a grant is, what about coaching? According to Wikipedia, the free encyclopedia, "Coaching" is training or development in which a person called a "coach" supports a learner in achieving a specific personal or professional goal. The learner is sometimes called a "coachee." Occasionally, "coaching" may mean an informal relationship between two people, of whom one has more experience and expertise than the other and offers advice and guidance as the later learns.

The following quote from Carter McNamara in his article, "All about Personal and Professional Coaching" (http://managementhelp.org/leadingpeople/coaching.htm), helps to clarify the coaching concept.

"Coaching involves working in a partnership between coach and clients to provide structure, guidance and support for clients to:

1. take a complete look at their current state, including their assumption and perception about their work, themselves and/or others;
2. set relevant and realistic goals for themselves, based on their own nature and needs;
3. take relevant and realistic actions toward reaching their goals; and
4. learn by continuing to reflect on their actions and sharing feedback with others along the way."

People usually think of coaching in terms of athletics. However, a variety of other areas also use coaches to increase skills and functioning. The concept of coaching has evolved to include life coaching, management coaching, wealth coaching, health coaching, and so on. Basically, coaching describes a process that transports people from where they are to where they want to be. Coaching is now such a popular concept that it is believed by many to have evolved into a discipline and is supported by organizations such as the Association for Coaching and the International Coach Federation.

Grants coaching is a relatively new application of the coaching concept and is aimed at helping grant seekers obtain grants that move them forward in their chosen fields and careers. Combining grants with coaching provides the grant seeker with a personal coach that uses a variety of techniques to develop the coachee into a highly effective grant seeker.

With funding rates of less than 10 percent at many government programs and foundations, and corporate-estimated success rates of 5–7 percent, the more than one million nonprofit organizations in the United States are desperate to learn techniques to increase their success rates and thus justify the time they spend grant seeking. Many nonprofits are already investing in one or more of the three major forms of assistance available in the grants field—grants training, grants consulting, and grants mentorship. Since there is little to no research on the efficiency of any of these strategies (including grants coaching), it is difficult for the serious grant seeker to determine which development strategy to employ. What might be helpful is determining how grants training, consulting, and mentorship differ from grants coaching.

GRANTS TRAINING

Grants training consists of an educational learning program where an individual possessing significant knowledge and/or experience presents subject matter on accessing and applying for foundation, corporate, and/or government grant opportunities. The training is usually in the form of a seminar designed to provide participants with techniques to access and secure grants more efficiently. Unlike grants coaching, this activity typically occurs in a group setting. Therefore, there is normally limited individual interaction.

GRANTS CONSULTING

While grants coaching is not usually aimed at solving a particular problem, grants consulting is. For example, a grant consultant may help individuals, teams, groups, or an entire organization develop one proposal to a specific grant program.

GRANTS MENTORSHIP

Many large nonprofit organizations employ a process whereby an individual with more extensive grants expertise works with newer (and possibly less experienced) staff to demonstrate how to do something he or she is really good at. The instruction is based on demonstrating or showing the mentee how the mentor approaches and completes grant-related tasks and often involves shadowing. Coaching differs from this in that it focuses on realizing and developing the skills that the grant seeker already has and augmenting them with new skills.

All of the aforementioned types of grant assistance have advantages as well as shortcomings. In my forty-five years in the field I have been involved in all of them in one form or another and have found that the major disadvantage to all of them is that they require extrapolation and internalization by the grant seeker. As a grant seeker, I was ultimately left with the task of determining how to apply what I was presented with into my grant-seeking strategies and career.

Although I personally was able to do this, I became aware that my seminar participants were not progressing and adapting the techniques I presented at a rate that was acceptable to me. I determined this by reviewing the follow-up evaluations I conducted in addition to the evaluations administered immediately after my seminars. While the evaluations from approximately thirty-five thousand participants showed me what my seminar attendees thought were valuable and useful steps contained in my curriculum and what I definitely should include in my books on successful grant-seeking strategies, the follow-up evaluations were more revealing. The follow-up evaluations demonstrated that my seminar participants often had difficulty adapting and adopting the strategies presented in the training.

After taking part in a national training labs workshop I was exposed to the concept of developing a "self-learning and improvement contract" and began to employ it in my grants training and consulting. This technique requires seminar participants to identify those grant-seeking strategies presented in the workshop that they feel would help them move their grant seeking forward and to list them on a two-part carbonless form known as a contract. I encourage them to list their steps in thirty-day increments to create a ninety-day contract for change. I instruct participants to keep one copy of their contract, place the other copy of their contract in an envelope I provide, and self-address it for return to them in ninety days whereupon they can check off the actions they completed.

My purpose in employing this self-learning contract concept is to increase the likelihood that my seminar participants will actually complete the steps they feel will impact their grants success. (Educational theory suggests that if an individual signs a contract with him or herself it becomes a demonstration of public commitment, which leads to an increased likelihood of compliance.)

While a small sampling of my seminar participants did show an increase in compliance, the amount of change was still not acceptable to me. In discussing this with an administrator at Western Michigan University (WMU), one of the institutions I was working with at the time, the administrator suggested that the university hire me to come back in ninety days to meet individually with each seminar participant. During this thirty-minute meeting we would open their contract envelopes together and review the completion of the tasks outlined on the contract. We would assess their progress in achieving their goals, work on defining their research/grants plan, and develop a new ninety-day contact. I would then return in another ninety days to repeat the process.

The WMU administrator phoned two weeks prior to my first ninety-day visit to report a considerable increase in grants activity by those faculty members who had developed ninety-day contracts during my initial seminar. They did not want to meet with me without having completed their work. The administrator was so impressed by their progress that she contracted with me for four more ninety-day campus visits over the course of one year. By the end of the contract period, 50 percent of the program participants were successful in attracting grant funding.

I realized that I was no longer just a grants trainer, consultant, and mentor but also a grants coach and began to change my business accordingly. I reduced my number of grants training seminars and concentrated on promoting long-term grants coaching contracts. I have now conducted grants coaching programs at universities across the United States, and program evaluations have consistently shown impressive success rates in securing grant funds. Because of these impressive success rates, more and more universities want grants coaching programs, and I suggest you consider implementing one at your organization.

Part I

THE GRANTS COACHING PROGRAM

Chapter One

Goals, Objectives, and Benefits

Federal appropriations will continue to experience reductions as a result of high deficits and budget rescissions. Because of this the current federal research/grants marketplace is pressured to do more with less funding. One result of this is a marketplace that encourages applicants (potential grantees) to develop consortia among nonprofit and profit entities to stay competitive and cost efficient. For your institution to increase its success rate and improve its effectiveness in this marketplace you must move away from reactive grants systems that are plagued by last-minute proposal preparation and employ a proactive grants program that is proven to achieve 50 percent success rates and higher. Implementing a grants coaching program is an ideal way to help you and your organization deal with marketplace realities and guarantee that your institution's resources and the time of your researchers and staff are used wisely.

Review the following sample goals and objectives. Refine the objectives and then compare them with your research/grants program's desired outcomes. Suggested measurement indicators and time frames are included in the objectives to enable you to measure your grant system's success. Compare increases in your grants success with the increased cost of any intervention you select to create improvement including the grants coaching program concept.

Your first step toward the development of your grants coaching program should be to identify the stated goals and objectives of your institution's research/grants program.

Common goals include:

- Increasing the quality and quantity of research/project proposals.
- Involving more faculty/staff in the grant-seeking process.
- Improving your institution's image in the grants marketplace through high-quality proposals and programs.
- Developing opportunities to further the mission of the institution through attracting grants, projects, research, and programs funded by sources outside the institution.
- Providing faculty and staff with the most current and productive tools/techniques to create winning proposals.

Sample objectives to achieve these goals include:

- To increase the number of faculty/staff involved in seeking external funding from *(current number or percent)* to *(number or percent)* in year 1 and *(number of percent)* in year 5.
- To increase the success rate of first-time grant seekers from *(current percent)* to *(percent)* in year 1 and *(percent)* in year 5.
- To improve the success rate for resubmittals from *(current percent)* to *(percent)* in year 1 and *(percent)* in year 5.
- To increase the number of proposals that have undergone a quality circle/mock review prior to submittal to the research office from *(current number or percent)* to *(number or percent)* in year 1 and *(number or percent)* in year 5.
- To increase the institution's image by attracting funding for research and model/innovative projects.
- To use grant funding to increase the quantity and quality of journal publications and related presentations by your institution's researchers at conferences and meetings.
- To increase the capturing of indirect costs from *(current level)* to *(level)* in year 1 to *(level)* in year 5.

By implementing the grants coaching program presented in this book, your institution will achieve some of the goals listed above and produce dramatic changes in some of its identified objectives. Be aware that this grants coaching program will require your grants system to change some of its current practices and embrace new concepts. For example, the program does require the use of a grants coach for one to two years to ensure the implementation of proactive grants strategies that lead to winning grants. While this may initially seem costly, just remember the return you will receive in terms of increased success in achieving your goals and objectives.

Use your goals and objectives to establish a metric that will allow you to track your institution's success in attracting more funding through a higher level of proposal acceptance. Also, evaluate your institution's success at increasing the willingness of your faculty and staff to become involved in a process that will achieve 50 percent and higher success rates.

The main benefit of implementing a grants coaching program is that it can have dramatic and long-lasting positive effects on your grants efforts. In particular, the quality circle component of the grants coaching program has the potential to positively impact your institution's goals and objectives for years to come. It has been my experience that once I train several groups of program participants in this proactive practice and they begin using it and benefiting from it, word spreads quickly throughout the institution, and faculty and staff who are not even in the grants coaching program decide to partake in quality circles so their proposals can also be improved prior to submittal. Ultimately, this results in higher-quality proposals and greater success rates. This is just one example of how the grants coaching program can result in positive change not just for the faculty and staff in the program but also for the entire organization!

Chapter Two

Proactive Grant Seeking

The Foundation for an Effective Grants Coaching Program

The grants coaching program presented in this book is based on a proactive grant-seeking system rather than a reactive system. In a reactive system, grant seekers invest a lot of time just prior to the deadline. This approach often results in last-minute general proposals that are not targeted or tailored to a specific grantor and often go unfunded. In a proactive system, grant seekers start the proposal development process early and put in small amounts of time throughout the process. This enables the grant seeker to conduct research on his or her potential grantor, tailor a proposal based on his or her research findings, and employ quality assurance techniques to increase his or her chances of success.

Last-minute, beat-the-clock proposals experience the highest rate of failure. As one federal program officer put it, "They call it a grants deadline because grant seekers die trying to make it." All proposals are logged in when they arrive electronically. The program officer also said that her twenty years of experience had shown her that proposals submitted at the last minute had the most errors and omissions. It is rare for a proposal created thirty days before the deadline to be funded unless it is a resubmittal of a rejected proposal. And even beginning the resubmittal process thirty to sixty days before the deadline leaves too little time to gather the data needed to successfully reframe it. Reacting to a deadline in one to two months simply does not allow enough time to do the background work needed to create a quality proposal. In reality, a successful grants system entails beginning the process between six months and a year or more before the submittal deadline.

My successful grants coaching program is based on the grants/proposal development system described in my book, *The "How To" Grants Manual*. The system consists of a set of proactive grant-seeking steps. *The "How To"* describes these steps in detail and provides other materials that you will find helpful in developing your own tailored grants coaching program. It explains proactive grant-seeking principles and practices and provides downloadable exhibits, worksheets, and checklists that keep grant seekers on track by focusing on beginning the process early so that they have time to complete all the steps that lead to success well before the deadline.

My grant-winning proposal development system has resulted in success rates as high as 83 percent and consistently over 50 percent for those in my grants coaching programs. When reviewing and evaluating other grants/proposal systems, take into consideration that a 83 percent success rate was achieved by an engineering college that used *The "How To" Grants Manual* and my *Winning Grants*[1] videotape series in what was a precursor to fully developing my grants coaching program. The proactive strategies outlined in the manual moved the college from a 17 percent success rate and $7 million in grants to an 83 percent success rate and over $20 million in grant funding. The dean of the college was rewarded with a vice president's job in the University of Alabama system and his department chairs moved on to become deans at other universities.

In evaluating the college's success the following two key strategies were revealed:

- support, encouragement, and funding for preproposal contact, and
- the incorporation of quality circles (mock reviews) before submittal.

The optimal use of these strategies is not possible when putting together a proposal just a few weeks prior to the deadline. The point is to avoid reactive grant seeking, act proactively, and control the grant-seeking process from the beginning to the end.

Because of my personality and background in education and psychology, I am always asking why. If the benefits of proactive grant seeking are obvious, why do grant seekers need so much help in this area? Why do some grant seekers waste time by continually using a last-minute proposal development strategy that is destined to fail while others adopt proactive grant-seeking strategies resulting in success? Is it because they are so overwhelmed with their current job responsibilities that they have no extra time to make preproposal contact or participate in a quality circle? Is it because they are so busy today that they keep reassigning critical grant-seeking tasks to tomorrow?

In a perfect world, I would like the fellows in my year-long grants coaching programs to have a reduced work load. But over the last ten years this has never been the case and probably never will be. So what does make my most successful fellows/coachees different? The answer to this question is that their grants coach has helped them to develop the ability to organize their time and defer their gratification. Prioritizing and performing tasks that may relate to securing grant funding six months away requires the ability to defer today's gratification for that future gratification that comes from securing a funded grant.

Although the pros in proactive grant seeking far outweigh the cons, there is one potential pitfall you should be aware of as you consider implementing a grants coaching program at your institution, and that is whether your organization's existing grants administration system can work hand in hand with your new program. Check with the office responsible for budget preparation, sign-off procedures, and so on to learn exactly how the submittal process is handled so that you can ascertain whether your proactive system will work effectively with theirs.

In one of my grants coaching contracts some of my fellows/coachees submitted their proposals to their institution's grants office several weeks prior to their proposals' federal deadline. They heard nothing from their grants office for weeks and then were contacted at the last minute with questions and problems. In one case, these last-minute issues (which could have been dealt with much earlier) actually resulted in a missed deadline. After investigation, I found that the grants/research office worked backward from the deadlines, thus giving proposals submitted at the last minute priority over the proposals from my fellows/coachees whose deadlines were several weeks away.

This was in direct conflict with what I was preaching to my coachees about how to increase their chances of success by submitting proposals early. Unfortunately, I was unsuccessful in getting the entire university system to change. It seems even the people in grants administration who complained about last-minute proposal submits were so used to dealing with them that they could not see the value of rewarding proactive grant seeking. Chapter 19 deals with this issue in greater detail and provides strategies for the early involvement of your grants administrators.

The success of the grants coaching program you implement at your institution will depend on many factors but one of the foremost is how well you convince your administration of the importance of proactive grant seeking and whether or not you can get them to support these grant-winning strategies and steps that require early action.

One of these very important steps and a key component of any successful grants coaching program is preproposal contact with potential grantors. Studies document that contact made before a proposal is constructed doubles the proposal's success rate. Your institution must consider how it will support the travel necessary to make this initial contact and to continue it. While a subsequent chapter will address the importance of preproposal contact, what is imperative for you to realize now is that your administration must be fully onboard and supportive of this activity (preproposal contact) and all the other major components of the proactive grants system and grant coaching program you are proposing.

NOTE

1. David G. Bauer, *Winning Grants II* (Produced by University of Nebraska Television in Cooperation with the American Council on Education).

Chapter Three

Target Population

Irrespective of whether the intention of your grants coaching program is to impact grant seeking at an educational institution, a nonprofit organization, or a profit-making group, you will need to start the process by determining what population of faculty/employees/staff to target and how to tailor the program to the target population's needs.

In major league sports, a significant variable in the success of the coach rests in the skill and ability of each player. The coach manages the players and is heavily involved in the recruitment process and identifying potential players' qualifications. In the end, the sports coach is evaluated on how successful his or her players are and how well he or she put together a winning team.

Like the sports coach, the grants coach is evaluated by how successful his or her coachees are at winning (i.e., attracting funded grants/research). However, the situation is different from that of the sports coach. The grants coach usually has little to say in who is selected to participate in the program. The institution and the administrators offering the grants coaching program believe they know best whom they want in the program. However, since the grants coach is the one who is ultimately accountable for the success of the coachees, you may want to include the grants coach you are planning to use in your discussions on participant selection.

I personally have had minimal involvement in the selection of the coachees in my grants coaching programs. For the most part, my only involvement in the process has been providing the decision makers with examples of the criteria selection used in my past grants coaching programs and making them aware of the importance of identifying the different groups of grant seekers at their institution. Ascertaining the various groups of grant seekers and potential grant seekers within your organization will help you determine the particular group that has the greatest chance of moving toward grants success and hence, whom to include in your grants coaching program.

Begin your selection process by looking at the following groups to determine which one(s) could best benefit from a grants coaching program.

Group 1: This group is composed of grant seekers who are currently successful.
Remember that keeping this group churning out winning proposals is critical to

your institution's/organization's success. Survey them to find out what they think they need to keep up their current level of grants success and what they could use to increase their productivity.

Group 2: This group includes grant seekers who have submitted proposals and been awarded grants in the past but not in the last three years. Survey them to find out what they think they need to get back in the game.

Group 3: These grant seekers have submitted proposals but have never been funded. Survey them to see what they think their reasons for failure are and what help they think they need to be successful in the grants marketplace.

Group 4: Individuals in this group have never submitted a proposal. They can be broken into two subgroups. Subgroup 1 consists of new faculty/staff/employees who have been at your institution/organization for one to five years. Subgroup 2 is composed of faculty/staff/employees who have been at your institution/organization for longer than five years. Both of these subgroups offer tremendous potential. However, to make them productive, they will require more investment of resources than groups one, two, and three. In addition, you should examine why they have not been involved in grant seeking. For example, if you are with an educational institution, does its criteria for tenure and promotion take into consideration grant productivity? Or does it focus on other activities like publishing, service, and community engagement?

If the grants coaching program is going to be implemented at a college or university, you will have to determine whether your target population is new, untenured faculty, or experienced, tenured faculty. Most of my grants coaching programs are for faculty and staff new to the institution. At the collegiate level, my programs have focused primarily on untenured faculty. This population group is usually motivated to use successful grant seeking to fund research or model/demonstration grants that are likely to lead to publications, promotions, and tenure.

New faculty/staff are willing to invest the extra effort need to be successful in proactive grant seeking to achieve their goals. Tenured or senior faculty/staff present a different challenge. They may require substantial incentives to motivate themselves to both join and complete a grants coaching program.

After three very successful grants coaching cohorts at a university that increased the amount of funded research with fewer proposal submittals (and a success rate of over 50 percent), the administration decided to run a program for tenured faculty. The university initiated the application process and the tenured faculty members who applied for and were eventually admitted to the program were either getting into grant seeking for the first time or planning to get back into the process.

After conducting and evaluating the program, the university was not pleased with the results. The tenured coachees performed poorly on the benchmarks/criterion for success when compared to the new faculty cohorts. Very few successfully completed the requirement to submit a proposal to both a public (government) and private (foundation and corporate) grantor. The majority of them failed to complete many of the proactive grant-seeking steps such as making preproposal contact with grantors and requesting funded proposals from previous grantees. In addition, they missed more of their mandatory one-on-one coaching sessions than the other cohorts missed and did not take advantage of the program incentives that involved funding for travel and summer stipends.

Of course, the problem could have been that I, as their grants coach, was unable to meet their needs. However, based on the program's evaluation, the sponsor did not think that was the case. The consensus was that the tenured group was not as motivated as the other groups and had work habits and commitments that precluded the time needed to get involved in productive grant seeking.

A concept paper written by the Dr. James McLean, the former dean of the College of Education at the University of Alabama, on grants scholar programs presents more "food for thought" on this new, nontenured faculty versus mature, tenured faculty issue.[1] Dr. McLean used grants coaching programs over a nine-year period to increase his college's external funding from $1.5 million to over $16.2 million. In this paper, he provides his valuable insights on what he believes to be the critical elements for success. One of his beliefs is that untenured faculty are so overwhelmed with their first few years of responsibilities that they cannot use the grants coaching program as efficiently as mature faculty.

I leave it to you to take all of these factors and opinions into consideration when selecting participants for your grants coaching program. Just be aware that your decision about who to include and exclude should be based on your institution's/organization's goals and objectives for your proposed grant coaching program and not solely on the evaluation results of or opinions related to any other program.

Knowing that each of the groups mentioned in this chapter have a different investment/return and diverse pressures on their performance, try to determine what each group requires to commit to increasing their grants productivity by practicing a proactive approach to winning grants. Once you identify the group(s) to focus on, you are ready to begin the individual selection/application process.

NOTE

1. James McLean, "Thoughts on Grants Scholar Programs" (December 2015).

Chapter Four

Program Outlines, Participant Incentives, Requirements/Benchmarks

Once you have determined your grants coaching program participants/target population:

- review and consider the education components of a successful grants coaching program;
- consider what incentives other programs have incorporated into their programs to encourage participation; and
- formulate the expectations/requirements that will be expected from your institution/organization's participants/coachees.

This chapter includes several grants coaching program outlines from various sponsor institutions that I have worked with. The point of including these program outlines is to help you develop a program unique to your organization, its goals and objectives, and your target population. Do not panic when you see that some of the programs contained participant incentives that were quite costly to the sponsoring institution. Some very successful grants coaching programs have not included any incentives except for the educational advantages of gaining specialized training in grantsmanship.

In addition, if you encourage the participation of several target populations, the actual program, incentives, and requirements for participants may differ by target group. As you analyze the program outlines you will see how some sponsors initially tailored their incentives to target faculty and then changed them when the target population shifted to staff members.

Exhibit 4.1 describes one of the first grants coaching programs I conducted. The first part of the program outline describes eligibility for faculty as well as professional/administrative staff.

The program incentives/awards section explains what the monetary incentives can be used for. One of the unique aspects of this program's incentives is the monetary contribution by the college or vice presidential unit that nominated the participating faculty or staff. In addition, the vice president for research provided extra funding for travel to make a preproposal visit to a federal grantor.

The program requirements/educational components section defines the activities the participants are required to complete, including:

- workshop attendance (In the first program offered, the workshops consisted of a two-day seminar on federal grants and a one-day seminar on foundation grants. In subsequent programs the workshop schedule included a one-day federal grants class, a one-day foundation grants class, a half-day class on team and consortia building, and a half-day training on quality circles. See chapter 5 for detailed descriptions of the seminar curriculums.)
- participation in four individual meetings with the program facilitator (grants coach)
- development of a mentoring relationship with a faculty/staff member at another institution
- partaking in two or more quality circle reviews of proposals
- submitting two proposals for federal support within a designated time frame
- presenting two interim reports to the vice president for research on specific dates (The interim reports consisted of copies of the ninety-day contracts developed with me over the program's one-year period.)

Your review of the other sections of this outline (exhibit 4.1), such as application, criteria, review process, and deadlines, will further help you establish the components of your own, tailored program.

Exhibit 4.2 provides an example of a public relations/marketing piece on another grants coaching program. Offered by Wake Forest University (WFU) and known as the *C*reative and *R*esearch *A*ctivities *Deve*lopment and *E*nrichment (CRADLE) initiative, this news piece was designed to inform the university population about WFU's upcoming fifth program cohort (http://inside.wfu.edu/2015/08/cradle-program-invests-in-faculty-and-grantsmanship/). This is included here to show you one way of marketing a grants coaching program.

Exhibit 4.3 is another example of a public relations/marketing piece designed to invite faculty members to participate in a grants coaching program. What is noteworthy about this particular fifteen-month grantsmanship program is that it is not offered through the University of Alabama's research office but through the university's College of Arts and Sciences dean's office. It outlines the attendance requirements as well as the application requirements, including a letter of agreement, a summary of the applicants' proposed research/creative activity, and a vitae.

Exhibit 4.4 is an outline of WFU's program and a call for applications. This program, unlike some of the other grants coaching programs, is a full two-year program and allows the participants/coachees not only to develop a proactive grant-seeking system but also to implement it beyond just applying for federal grants. The program provides for significant follow-up coaching for dealing with the award and rejection of proposals. In addition, it allows for refining the participant's one- and five-year grants career plans. When reviewing the program description, note that the $5,000 stipend under the award section is awarded for summer work over two summers and is contingent on workshop attendance and meeting the other participation requirements.

Research Development Award Program

The Research Development Award Program assists early-career faculty and staff in vice presidential areas in advancing their research plans by providing a series of development activities designed to facilitate the process of securing federal funding for their projects. Under the conditions of the program, the vice president for research makes as many as 20 awards annually.

Eligibility

Eligible faculty members are all bargaining-unit members in a tenured or tenured-track appointment (a) whose date of hire is between July 1, ____, and August 31, ____, (b) who will have completed at least two academic terms by the start of the program, and (c) who demonstrate interest in grant seeking through such means as submission of proposals for external funding, submission of proposals for internal funding, or serving in some role on funded projects. Previous Research Development Award recipients may not re-apply. Eligible professional/administrative staff are those P-level appointments in vice presidential administrative areas who demonstrate interest in grant seeking. Staff may have also enrolled in proposal writing workshops, assisted in gathering data for a proposal, served as reviewers for proposals, or been employed in some role on funded projects.

Program Incentives/Awards

The vice president for research will award each RDA faculty and staff member $____, established in a research account to support expenses related to grant seeking and research. The award shall be used for travel to visit a mentor. In addition, equipment, student employees, postage, and supplies are examples of approved uses of the award; salary for the RDA faculty or staff member is not. In addition, the college or vice presidential unit will award each of its participating faculty or staff $____, in the same manner and for the same purpose. Finally the vice president for research will support one visit to a federal sponsor by the RDA participant; the amount, not to exceed $____, shall reimburse transportation and lodging expenses.

Program Requirements/Educational Components

RDA program participants agree to complete the following program activities during the period May ____ through December ____:

1. A two-day workshop on seeking and winning federal grants.
2. A one-day workshop on seeking foundation grants.
3. Four individual meetings with the RDA program workshop facilitator, to define a research plan and assess progress in achieving goals.
4. Develop a mentoring relationship with a faculty or staff member at another institution in order to establish a network of key colleagues. At least one meeting with the mentor shall occur on the mentor's campus.
5. Participate in two or more quality circle reviews of proposals.
6. Submit two proposals for federal support before December ____.
7. Submit interim reports on December 15, ____, and April 30, ____ to the vice president for research.

Exhibit 4.1 Sample Grants Coaching Program Outline: Research Development Award Program.

Application

Deans will notify eligible faculty members, and vice presidents will notify eligible staff members to invite application for the FY____-____ competition. All applications are made to the appropriate dean or vice president.

The application consists of:

1. A description of the research problem for which funding is being sought, including its significance, a brief review of current research or programs in the area, the scope of work necessary to address the problem, and the result or benefit to society (three pages maximum);
2. A statement of sponsored funding goals, quantified by number of proposals and award amounts, for three years beginning in ____-____ (one page maximum);
3. Evidence of demonstrated interest in research and grant seeking (e.g., proposals submitted, member of grant review panel, publications in refereed journals, theses or dissertations advised, professional service as editor of journal) (one page maximum); and
4. Expertise profile available on the Community of Science database or equivalent.

Criteria for Admission into the Research Development Award Program

Applications of merit will demonstrate that:

1. Study of the proposed research problem advances the research plans of the college or unit.
2. The research is feasible, given available fiscal, physical, and human resources.
3. Federal funding exists for the proposed research.
4. Interest in grant seeking convincingly demonstrates likelihood of full RDA program participation.
5. The applicant's academic preparation and experience indicate appropriate expertise.

Review Process

Deans and vice presidents will solicit RDA applications from a pool of eligible applicants that they identify (deans will identify faculty, vice presidents will identify professional/administrative staff). Deans and vice presidents will then review their college or unit applications according to the criteria and forward to the vice president for research a rank-ordered listing of applications for funding and copies of the proposals. In the event that the number of applications exceeds the number of awards available, the vice president for research reserves the right to determine distribution of awards.

Deadlines

Proposals for FY ____-____ awards must be submitted to the dean or appropriate vice president no later than _ p.m. on _____. Applications are due in the Office of the Vice President for Research on _____. Awards will be announced on _____. Please direct questions to _____ at ___-____.

Exhibit 4.1 (*continued*)

Exhibit 4.5 is an example of a grants coaching program application. This particular application is used by WFU and requires the applicant to provide a description of his or her proposed area of research or other creative activity. A two-page vitae and signatures from the applicant, department chair/director, and dean are also required.

Both program outlines provided thus far (exhibits 4.1 and 4.4) call for individual meetings/interviews with the grants coach. Exhibit 4.6 is an example of a sign-up sheet that can be used to schedule forty-five-minute participant/coach one-on-one meetings. Exhibit 4.7 is an example of sign-up that can be used to schedule sixty-minute meetings. Irrespective of the length of the individual meetings, the participant/coachees are asked to commit to his or her next one-on-one meeting that will occur in thirty, sixty, or ninety days, depending on the program's requirements/components.

Inside WFU

Wake Forest News for faculty and staff

CRADLE program invests in faculty and grantsmanship

August 13, 2015

The Creative Research Activities Development and Enrichment (CRADLE) initiative is engaging with its fifth cohort of faculty this September and continues to experience interest and success.

The Office of the Provost and the Office of Research and Sponsored Programs (ORSP) coordinate the program. CRADLE aims to develop competitive external proposals that support multiyear research projects and creative activities. Fellows receive assistance from both internal and external consultants to improve their grantsmanship and to articulate a five-year career plan that incorporates proven strategies for developing and funding superior research and creative activities.

"We began CRADLE because we wanted to help faculty develop competitive grant proposals," said Lori Messer, director of ORSP.

On Sept. 18, the new cohort will attend the first of four seminars, "Winning Grants," that will cover federal grants. In December, another seminar focused on foundation and corporate grants will be held. Other CRADLE sessions will focus on quality and team building. Participants also work one-on-one with a grants consultant to develop 90-day contracts that outline their grant plans.

The seminars are open to non-CRADLE participants.

Messer, along with Amy Comer, associate director, and Stephen Williams, assistant director of research and sponsored programs, have given regional and national presentations about the CRADLE program, most recently for the National Council of University Research Administrators to highlight the need of the program.

"We're inspiring other universities to do this, to start their own programs," Messer said.

Former CRADLE participant Wayne Pratt, associate professor of psychology, appreciated how the program ad its consultants demonstrated patience in meeting him where he was at in the grant writing process.

"Under CRADLE's guidance, I was able to research potential funding mechanisms, learn which were most competitive for my own situation, and determine what preliminary steps I needed to take in order to have the best chances at successful grantsmanship," he said. "I never felt pushed or rushed into submitting until I was ready to, and I appreciated the support from both the program and my CRADLE colleagues that ultimately led to a successful application!"

The CRADLE program can also boast that four former participants – Timo Thonhauser and Oana Jurchescu from the physics department, and Amanda Jones and Patricia Dos Santos from the chemistry department – have all been awarded National Science Foundation Career Awards.

Dos Santos was a CRADLE fellow in her second year on faculty. She credits the program consultant for helping to "identify a path for success" with grant writing because "it is not about quantity but the quality of proposals being submitted" that makes a difference.

"The program provided structure for my efforts in grant seeking and writing. I have valued the support from ORSP staff in assisting a junior (and senior) faculty with the complications of putting together a budget and editing the proposal to a language that is appealing to certain granting agencies," she said. "I'm aware that this is not a standard practice at other institutions, and I appreciate the investment that Wake is making in junior faculty so that they can succeed in their grantsmanship."

Exhibit 4.2 Sample Public Relations/Marketing Piece.

> **The University of Alabama – College of Arts & Science**
>
> The College of Arts & Sciences is pleased to offer for the fifth year an exciting opportunity for all faculty members to enhance their grantsmanship skills. Interested faculty members may apply to be part of a 15-month training program with well-known, external funding expert David G. Bauer. At the successful completion of the program, each participant will have researched, drafted, and submitted a proposal for funding.
>
> Participation is open to all <u>tenured</u> and <u>tenure-track</u> faculty. In 2015, the following meeting dates will take place:
>
> - First day-long seminar for 2015 cohort participants, **January 6**.
> - 1-on-1 meetings with Mr. Bauer for 2015, **January 7– 9** (Sign-up for time slot at seminar).
> - Second day-long seminar for 2015 cohort participants, **March 26**.
> - 1-on-1 meetings with Mr. Bauer for 2015 cohorts, **March 27, 30, 31** (Sign-up for time slot at seminar).
> - Final 1-on-1 meetings with Mr. Bauer for 2014 cohort participants, **March 23-25**.
> - Graduation Luncheon for 2014 cohort participants, **March 25**, Cypress Inn. 2015 cohort participants will also be invited to attend. Dean's Office will send out RSVP email to participants.
> - 1-on-1 Meetings with Mr. Bauer for 2015 cohort participants, **June 8-10** (Sign up for slot in March)
>
> The 3rd and 4th seminars are planned for August 2015 and December 2015. These seminars will also be followed by 1-on-1 meetings. Continued participation in the program will depend on strict attendance at the seminars and attainment of established milestones. This means that you will likely have to make alternative arrangements for your courses on 2-3 days during the year.
>
> To participate, faculty members should contact their chairs to ensure his/her support. To register for the training program faculty must submit the following:
>
> 1. **Letter of agreement signed by you and your department chair.**
> 2. **A one-page summary of your proposed research/creative activity.**
> 3. **Your vitae.**
>
> These items should be submitted by the faculty member to _____ by **December 12, 2014**.
>
> Questions about the program should be directed to the Senior Associate Dean, College of Arts & Sciences.

Exhibit 4.3   Sample Invitation to Participate in a Grants Coaching Program.

Exhibit 4.8 is a sample of program agreement that outlines the obligations of the faculty members participating in the University of Alabama's College of Arts and Sciences grantsmanship training program and the support to be provided by the college. It provides a timeline and the benchmarks the participants must achieve to receive the benefits provided by the program.

Exhibit 4.9 is an example of an invitation sent by the University of Alabama, College of Arts & Sciences to a graduation luncheon for those program participants/coachees who have successfully met their program's benchmarks. An invitation is also sent to coachees in the college's current program who are still working on meeting their benchmarks. The purpose of the current coachees' attendance is so they can hear the graduates' thoughts on the most valuable parts of the program. The graduates also report on their progress such as grants awarded, pending applications, and the resulting publications.

CRADLE CREATIVE AND RESEARCH ACTIVITIES DEVELOPMENT AND ENRICHMENT INITIATIVE V

The Office of the Provost and the Office of Research and Sponsored Programs (ORSP) invite applications for the 2015 CRADLE V initiative. Up to 10 fellows will be selected to participate for two years, beginning in fall 2015, with preference to tenure-track faculty.

Purpose

CRADLE aims to develop competitive external proposals to support multiyear research projects and creative activities. Fellows will receive assistance from both internal and external consultants to improve their grantsmanship and to articulate a 5-year career plan that incorporates proven strategies for developing and funding superior research and creative activities.

Award

Fellows will receive group and individual training with grants consultant David Bauer over the two-year period as well as assistance from ORSP staff. They will also receive a $5K summer stipend to focus on the program, half in the summer between the first and second years and the other half at the end of the second year, as well as $1K travel supplement. Receipt of the stipend is contingent on workshop attendance and participation each year.

Program

Fellows will contract with the Office of the Provost and ORSP to participate as follows:

September 2015

- Attend part one of an intensive two-part grants seminar (federal grant seeking)
- Participate in an individual interview with the grants consultant to clarify proposal agenda and professional development plan (PDP)

December 2015

- Attend part two of an intensive two-part grants seminar (foundation and corporate grant seeking)
- Participate in an individual interview with the grants consultant to review progress on the PDP
- Develop a project outline for approval as potentially fundable by the grants consultant
- Identify three top scholars in the field who might be approached for proposal review

April 2016

- Participate in a half-day seminar on Quality Circles*
- Participate in an individual interview with the grants consultant to review and adapt PDP strategies
- Establish phone or email contact with at least one scholar who will serve as a proposal mentor
- Refine white paper into 5-10 page scope of work
- Identify potential funding sources and develop letters of inquiry, making site visits to top scholars and funding sources as necessary

Participants will be expected to put their proposals through a quality circle improvement exercise and assist other CRADLE Fellows by acting as participant reviewers or a quality circle leader

Exhibit 4.4 Sample Grants Coaching Program Outline and Call for Applications: CRADLE Initiative.

> Summer 2016
>
> - Develop full proposal for submission to funding source
> - Have proposal reviewed by proposal mentor
> - Have proposal reviewed and approved by grants consultant
> - Make site visits to top scholars and funding sources as necessary
>
> September 2016
>
> - Participate in an individual interview with the grants consultant
> - Participate in a half-day seminar on Forming Productive Groups and Teams
> - Refine and submit proposals not submitted in the summer
>
> December 2016
>
> - Participate in an individual interview with the grants consultant
> - Discuss proposal reviews/feedback as received
> - Refine and resubmit proposals for funding
>
> September 2017
>
> - Participate in an individual interview with the grants consultant
> - Discuss proposal reviews/feedback as received
> - Refine and submit proposals for funding
>
> Application forms (attached) should be submitted electronically by 5 P.M. on 27 March 2015. Applicants will be notified of selection in May 2015.

Exhibit 4.4 (*continued*)

Exhibit 4.10 is an example of the University of Alabama's Certificate of Completion for its eighteen-month Research Fellowship Program on advanced grant-seeking skills. The College of Arts and Sciences also provides a certificate of completion for quality circle/mock review training. The participants/coachees can list these certificates on their vitae. In one case, a coachee who listed his quality circle training on his vitae was hired at another university under the stipulation that he teach a quality circle seminar at his new place of employment.

Exhibit 4.11 outlines the educational components and timeline for a grants coaching program offered by the University of North Carolina Greensboro (UNCG). What makes this program particularly unique is that it applies the grants coaching concept to graduate students. It was developed by Dr. William Wiener as a result of his success with a grants coaching program his office sponsored at Marquette University. Dr. Wiener was in charge of research and grants at Marquette as well as functioning as the dean of the graduate school.

The grants coaching program he adopted at Marquette emphasized the use of quality circles to improve proposals prior to submittal. The program was credited with doubling the university's external funding. When Dr. Wiener accepted the position of dean of graduate studies at UNCG, he requested that I work with him again on a grants coaching program focused on graduate students.

The program for graduate students is somewhat different from other grants coaching programs I have conducted. Basically, it is a condensed version of my other programs. It provides the graduate students with four one-half-day grants-related seminars instead of one- or two-day seminars and thirty-minute one-on-one meetings instead of

WAKE FOREST UNIVERSITY

Office of Research and Sponsored Programs

CREATIVE AND RESEARCH ACTIVITIES DEVELOPMENT AND ENRICHMENT (CRADLE) INITIATIVE – 2015-2017 Fellowship Application

Name: _____

Department or School: _____

Brief Description of proposed area of research or other creative activity:

_____

Please attach 2-page CV

If selected as a CRADLE V Fellow, I commit to meeting the obligations described in the call for applications. I understand that receipt of program stipend each summer is contingent on attendance and participation in required workshops:

_____   _____
Applicant's Signature   Date

If the applicant noted above is selected as a CRADLE V Fellow, we agree to assist him/her in meeting the program requirements throughout the two-year period, beginning September 2015:

_____   _____
Department Chair/Director's Signature   Date

_____   _____
Dean's Signature   Date

Exhibit 4.5 Sample Grants Program Application.

1-on-1 Meetings	
Location:	
Date:	
8:00-8:45 am	
8:50-9:35 am	
9:40-10:25 am	
10:25-10:45 am	Break
10:45-11:30 am	
11:35-12:20 pm	
12:20-1:15 pm	Lunch
1:15-2:00 pm	
2:05-2:50 pm	
2:55-3:40 pm	
3:45-4:00 pm	Break
4:00-4:45 pm	
4:50-5:35 pm	

Exhibit 4.6 Sample Forty-Five-Minute Sign-Up Sheet.

1-on-1 Meetings	
Location:	
Date:	
8:00-9:00 am	
9:00-10:00 am	
10:00-10:30 am	Break
10:30-11:30 am	
11:30-12:30 am	
12:30-1:30 pm	Lunch
1:30-2:30 pm	
2:30-3:00 pm	Break
3:00-4:00 pm	
4:00-5:00 pm	

Exhibit 4.7 Sample Sixty-Minute Sign-Up Sheet.

> **2016 Program Agreement**
>
> **College of Arts and Sciences Grantsmanship Training**
>
> This agreement outlines both the obligations of the faculty member participating in the College of Arts and Sciences Grantsmanship Training program and the support to be provided by the College. The program begins in January 2016 and ends in April 2017.
>
> As long as the benchmarks are achieved, the College of Arts and Sciences will provide the following benefits for faculty participating in the program over the one year period.
>
> 1. specialized training in grantsmanship, and
> 2. access to an expert external grant mentor during the course of the program.
>
> The following timeline and benchmarks apply to faculty participating in the program:
>
> - January 2016 - attend all training offered; participate in individual review with the grant consultant;
> - March 2016 – describe research agenda; identify at least 3 top researchers in the field; have research agenda approved by external expert as potentially fundable;
> - August 2016 – refine initial description into 5 to 10 page scope of work; establish telephone contact with at least 1 of the top three researchers identified; develop a foundation inquiry letter; identify at least 3 potential funding sources; have face-to-face meeting with the grant consultant; have telephone and e-mail contact with the grant consultant as needed; contact at least one funding agency about possible funding; identify a funding source to which you will apply for funds;
> - December 2016 – have face-to-face meeting with the grant consultant; develop full proposal for submission to potential funding source; telephone/e-mail consultation available with grant expert as needed; have the proposal reviewed and approved by an outside expert;
> - April 2017 – face-to-face meeting with grant consultant as necessary; luncheon reception.
>
> Failure to meet one or more of the benchmarks in a timely manner may result in being dropped from the program. In such as case, none of the benefits would be available past the time at which the benchmark was not met.
>
> Accepted:
>
> _____   _____
> Faculty Member Signature   Date   Department Chair Signature   Date
>
>
> _____   _____
> Faculty Rank/Title   Email   Phone
>
>
> _____
> Dean Signature   Date

Exhibit 4.8 Sample Grants Coaching Program Agreement.

forty-five- or sixty-minute sessions. (Note that the individual meetings are scheduled via doodle polls.) In addition, the program is just eight months long to accommodate the students' need to find and obtain funding for the next academic year. This shorter program also calls for less investment of consulting time and thus reduces program costs.

> # THE UNIVERSITY OF ALABAMA
> COLLEGE OF ARTS AND SCIENCES
>
> *Dean* _____
>
> *Invites you to the*
>
> *Bauer Grant Writing Graduation Luncheon*
>
> *Thursday March 26th, 2015*
>
> *12:00 p.m. to 2:00 p.m.*
>
> *Hotel Capstone*
>
> *320 Paul W Bryant Drive*
>
> *Tuscaloosa, AL 35401*
>
> *Please RSVP by*
>
> *Friday March 20th, 2015*

Exhibit 4.9 Sample Invitation to Graduation Luncheon.

Another component of this program is that the graduate students are encouraged to involve their mentors/academic advisors. Their mentors/advisors are allowed and encouraged to attend all of the grants workshops but especially to the session focusing on quality circles. This has been such a success that the 2015–2016 program consists of an additional day and a half of quality circles. During this day and a half each program participant has a mock review of his or her draft proposal and each mentor/academic advisor is encouraged to attend his or her student's review. The 2015–2016 program has already seen a substantial increase in faculty/advisor participation, so much so that faculty are now requesting a grants coaching program of their own!

Exhibit 4.12 outlines my newest grants coaching program sponsored by the University of Alabama's Division of Community Affairs. This innovative use of grants

> **College of Arts & Sciences**
>
> **The University of Alabama**
>
> **CERTIFICATE OF COMPLETION**
>
> This certificate is awarded to
>
> **NAME**
>
> For completing the 18 month research Fellowship Program
> on advanced grant seeking skills
>
> **Awarded this 26th day of April, 2015**
>
> Dr. _____, Dean David G. Bauer, President
> The College of Arts and Sciences David G. Bauer Associates, Inc.

Exhibit 4.10 Sample Certificate of Completion.

> The UNCG Graduate School
>
> 2014-15 Research Development Program
>
> a. September, 2014
>
> i. Monday, 9/15/14 – ½ day Prestigious Awards for Student Support Seminar, 8:00 – 12:00
> ii. Monday afternoon, 9/15/14 or Tuesday, 9/16/14 – meet individually with expert for 30 minutes. This will be scheduled via Doodle Poll in August
>
> b. December, 2014
>
> i. Thursday, 12/4/14 – ½ day Federal Grants Seminar, 8:00 – 12:00
> ii. Thursday afternoon, 12/4/14 or Friday, 12/5/14 – meet individually with expert for 30 minutes. This will be scheduled in the Fall.
>
> c. January, 2015
>
> i. Thursday, 1/22/15 – ½ day Foundation and Corporate Grants Seminar, 8:00 – 12:00
> ii. Thursday afternoon 1/22/15, or Friday, 1/23/15 – meet individually with expert for 30 minutes. This will be scheduled via Doodle Poll in the Fall.
>
> d. April, 2015
>
> i. Tuesday, 4/7/15 – ½ day quality circle seminar, 8:00 – 12:00 Note: This requires the participation of the mentor as well as the participant.
> ii. Tuesday afternoon, 4/7/15 or Wednesday, 4/8/15 – meet individually with expert for 30 minutes. This will be scheduled via Doodle Poll in the Early Spring.

Exhibit 4.11 Sample Grants Coaching Program: Research Development Program.

Grant Acquisition Program

University of Alabama Community Affairs

Workshop I: Winning Government Grants, 8:30 a.m. – 4:30 p.m.

Coaching Session 1

Workshop II: Winning Foundation/Corporate Grants, 8:30 a.m. – 4:30 p.m.

Coaching Session 2

Benchmarks

- Definition of problem or situation that prompted program
- Description of desired or optimal state
- Description of what exists now
- Gap: Difference between "ideal" and "current"
- Brief description of program to bridge tap
- List of potential funders
- Report of pre-proposal contact for at least one potential funder

Workshops III and IV: Team Building and Quality Circles (Mock Reviews), 9 a.m. –12 p.m., 1 p.m. – 4 p.m.

Coaching Session 3

Benchmarks

- Report of additional funders including foundations and corporations
- Report of pre-proposal contact of foundation or corporation if applicable
- Share proposal concept paper with grant coach
- Have obtained copies of related proposals that were funded successfully

Workshop V: Sustaining Programs through Fundraising, 8:30 a.m. – 4:30 p.m.

Coaching Session 4

Benchmarks

- Have created advisory group
- Have a draft of a proposal to be used in quality circle (mock review)

Coaching Session 5

Benchmarks

- Have a refined draft of proposal
- Have developed a sustainability plan

General Program Information

This winning grants program focuses on the training of teams rather than individuals and includes a sustainability component that calls for obtaining grants to implement and evaluate the teams' projects/programs. Team projects/programs must address a community need. Each team must consist of at least one university faculty or staff member and one community person. Applicants for this program are required to submit an abstract of the project/program they want to find funding for. The abstract should describe the project/program including the need and solution. All team members must commit to attending the four days of workshops and the five coaching sessions over the 15-month program period and agree to meet each coaching session's benchmarks.

Exhibit 4.12   Sample Grants Coaching Program Outline: Grants Acquisition Program.

coaching focuses on community engagement and is aimed at developing leaders in the art of funding and sustaining university/community research partnerships. The program, organized by Dr. Samory T. Pruitt, vice president for the Division of Community Affairs, and Dr. James E. McLean, executive director of the Center for Community-Based Partnerships, takes grants coaching to a new level by using the concept to empower ten University of Alabama/community teams to discover ways to fund their essential activities. This grant acquisition/grants coaching program represents a unified effort to bring the University of Alabama campus and the community together to solve problems of mutual interest. Review this inventive program's workshop and coaching session benchmarks to determine if any of them could be tailored to your program.

When studying the various aspects of the different program outlines presented in this chapter and identifying the components (i.e., incentives, benchmarks, and so on) that could be used in your program, take into consideration the following variables:

- overall length of the program (i.e., twelve months, fifteen months, eighteen months, and so on);
- number of grants seminars, content, and length of each (i.e., half a day, one day, two days, and so on);
- number of coaching sessions, time between coaching sessions (i.e., thirty days, sixty days, ninety days, and so on), length of time for each individual meeting (i.e., thirty minutes, forty-five minutes, sixty minutes, and so on);
- the role of the coach between the seminars and one-on-one meetings/visits (i.e., e-mail/phone/Skype contact, proposal review, and so on).

After you review the program outlines and their incentives and requirements (referred to as benchmarks by some sponsors), develop a draft of your proposed grants coaching program. Provide a copy of it to several members of your target population to get their feedback. What you would like to know is whether they would be interested in applying to such a program if it was offered. You would also like their opinions on the proposed requirements and incentives and their suggestions on how the program could be improved.

Chapter Five

Educational Components

After reviewing the various grants coaching program outlines in chapter 4, you can see that all of the institutions/organizations I have worked with include the following two educational components in their programs:

- training seminars to increase the participants' knowledge of the grants marketplace and proactive grant-seeking strategies, and
- individual meetings with the program participants to define research plans, set goals, and access their progress in achieving their goals.

When developing your program, I suggest you include a series of seminars. The grants coaching programs developed by my sponsors include four seminar sessions usually occurring within a 1–1½-year time frame. They include:

- How to Find—and Win—Government Grants;
- How to Find—and Win—Foundation and Corporate Grants;
- Keys to Increasing Collaboration and Effective Team Building; and
- Improving Grant Proposals through Quality Circles.

The government grants seminar and the foundation and corporate grants seminar are usually one full day each. The team-building seminar and the quality circle seminar are half a day each.

I encourage you to design your program so that it starts with the government grants seminar. Exhibit 5.1 provides an outline of this seminar. Part 2 of *The "How To" Grants Manual* provides more strategies on accessing public/government funding opportunities. The reason my sponsors start their programs off with this seminar is

> ### How to Find – And Win – Government Grants
>
> Get an insider's look at the government grants marketplace and find out how to locate the federal, state and block grants that are right for your organization. Your faculty and staff will learn where the money is, how funding decisions are made, and what a winning government proposal looks like.
>
> Participants will leave this seminar with:
> - a strategy for dealing with block grants and new federal programs
> - methods for researching government grant opportunities including the use of the Internet
> - ways to develop more fundable ideas
> - information on how to make pre-proposal contact with feds
> - ideas on how to use advocates to make grant seeking more efficient
> - knowledge of what it takes to prepare a grant winning government application
> - a sample federal composite application
> - a grants office time line
> - a sample federal grant reviewing exercise
> - a project planner to help develop budgets and cash forecasts
> - a way to improve proposals before submission
>
> Seminar materials include handouts and worksheets aimed at winning more government grants and *The "How To" Grants Manual: Successful Grantseeking Techniques for Obtaining Public and Private Grants.*

Exhibit 5.1 Seminar Outline: How to Find—And Win—Government Grants.

because they know that the federal government has $500 billion to distribute while foundations and corporations have only 10 percent of that amount. However, they also know that it is not just about the larger pot of money.

Savvy program sponsors realize that even if their program participant/coachee thinks his or her grant is not likely to receive federal support, he or she still needs to go to the public marketplace first to be told that his or her proposal does not fit the government's program. The program participant/coachee can then use his or her government rejection as one of the reasons to seek private grants.

Exhibit 5.2 provides an outline of my foundation and corporate grants seminar. Part 3 of *The "How To" Grants Manual* provides more strategies on accessing private/foundation funding opportunities. After analyzing the government grants marketplace, most program participants/coachees find themselves forced to realistically examine their chances of successfully playing the grants game at the public level. If they know they need preliminary data, larger number of subjects, or more publications to succeed at the government level, they may realize that the foundation and corporate marketplace is the best place to find the smaller grants that will eventually make them more fundable to government sources.

Once your program participants/coachees have the government grants and foundation and corporate grants seminars under their belts, it is time to move on to team and consortia building. Exhibit 5.3 outlines this seminar. Chapter 9 of *The "How*

How to Find – And Win – Foundation & Corporate Grants

Gain the specialized knowledge your organization needs to be a winner in the competitive private sector. Pare down the nation's more than 33 million companies and 100,000 foundations to those whose funding efforts match your organization's objectives.

This seminar will provide intensive instruction on how to tap into the $58 billion available in foundation grants and the $18 billion available in corporate grants. It will also provide step-by-step essentials for organizing and writing a successful foundation or corporate grant proposal. Your faculty and staff will learn how to:

- Research foundation and corporate funding sources
- Develop creative ideas that will attract more funding
- Use valuable time-saving techniques to make grant seeking controllable
- Locate grant opportunities through the Internet
- Use federal funding to win private funding
- Contact private funders
- Develop a checklist to get the complete funding picture in one phone call
- Harness community involvement and support
- Draft a compelling letter proposal containing the 9 key points for grants success
- Use webbing and linkages to develop inside leads to improve chances for funding
- Develop a way to improve proposals before submission
- Use a project planner to help develop budgets and cash forecasts

Seminar materials include handouts with valuable tips and strategies for private sector grants success and *The "How to" Grants Manual: Successful Grantseeking Techniques for Obtaining Public and Private Grants.*

Exhibit 5.2 Seminar Outline: How to Find—And Win—Foundation and Corporate Grants.

To" Grants Manual delves into this area in detail. The research I have conducted on my general seminar population enticed me to encourage my sponsors to include this team-building component in their programs. Less than 20 percent of my seminar participants have ever had formal training in how to work in groups. Unfortunately, the nonprofit marketplace is far behind the corporate world when it comes to developing these essential team skills.

The final seminar I suggest including in your grants coaching program is how to improve grant proposals through quality circles. Exhibit 5.4 provides an outline of this seminar. Basically, it consists of an explanation of what a quality circle is, why it is beneficial, and guidelines for conducting one. Chapters 16 and 25 of *The "How To" Grants Manual* provide an in-depth look at improving federal, foundation, and corporate proposals through the use of quality circles.

All of my sponsors have also chosen to include one-on-one meetings as part of their programs. These individual sessions are conducted after the seminars and are usually scheduled for forty-five or sixty minutes each. (Exhibits 4.6 and 4.7 in chapter 4 provide sample sign-up sheets.) During these face-to-face meetings

---

Keys to Increasing Collaboration and Effective Team Building

More and more grants and contracts are interdisciplinary and require collaboration among key, internal personnel. Others utilize external collaborations and consortia between other institutions, and even for-profit corporations.

This half day seminar is designed to assist faculty and staff members evaluate the skills they bring to a team effort or collaborative situation. In this seminar, participants will learn how to:

- evaluate groups roles and behavior,
- assess their team building skills,
- avoid behavior that is counter-productive to effective group functioning,
- develop new skills to improve their group performance,
- select group members, and
- assign tasks in a way that capitalizes on the skills of all of the group members.

The participants' investment of time in this seminar will have beneficial returns in their grant related productivity and their work with:

- department committees,
- undergraduate and graduate student groups,
- professional organizations,
- social service clubs, and
- community organizations.

This seminar incorporates stimulating activities and discussions to provoke introspection, insight, and personal learning. Materials include handouts developed especially for the seminar as well as a commercially produced, self-discovery tool.

Exhibit 5.3   Seminar Outline: Keys to Increasing Collaboration and Effective Team Building.

I work with the program participants to clarify their professional development plans, strategize how they can best meet their funding goals, and discuss their grant-seeking progress, problems, and so on. I also provide them with the dates for our next session of meetings and have them sign up for their desired time slot. That way, they can record their next one-on-one meetings in their personal calendars well in advance.

Improving Grant Proposals through Quality Circles

In this one-half day seminar your grant seekers will learn how to put their federal, state, foundation and corporate proposals through a quality circle before submittal. This process will promote quality in your grants program and dramatically improve your organization's grants success. Your organization's image with reviewers and grantors will also be enhanced by incorporating this concept into your proposal process.

Seminar participants will learn how to:

- evaluate their proposals using the actual review system they will encounter,
- identify the areas of their proposals that are weak and improve them to increase their scores,
- eliminate proposal errors and other elements that cost points, and
- make their proposals more readable from the grantor's perspective.

They will also learn how to set up and conduct a grants quality circle exercise to improve their colleagues' proposals before submission. Participants will leave this seminar with the skills necessary to:

- develop a quality circle setting and provide and maintain a positive atmosphere throughout the exercise,
- establish the parameters for the scoring system to be used and the time spent reading each proposal section,
- assist the quality circle participants in role playing the actual reviewers based on reviewer backgrounds, viewpoints, and biases,
- get everyone in the quality circle to participate and provide their opinions.
- handle group members who may not follow the quality circle guidelines, and
- keep the group on time and task.

Materials include handouts with all the forms and worksheets needed to participate in and lead effective quality circle exercises.

Exhibit 5.4   Seminar Outline: Improving Grant Proposals through Quality Circles.

Now that you are aware of the educational components included in the grants coaching programs I have facilitated, pick and choose what you would like to include in your program and determine how to tailor the seminars' contents and the individual meeting/interview agendas to fit your particular institution's/organization's needs.

Chapter Six

Estimating the Costs Associated with Your Unique Grants Coaching Program

The grants coaching program outlines in chapter 4 provide you with the educational components, incentives, and benchmarks included in some of the programs I have facilitated. You now have plenty of ideas on how your program *could* be structured and what it *could* include. Obviously, you want to develop a grants coaching program unique to your institution/organization. But what about cost effectiveness? How you structure your program and what elements you include in it will determine how much it will cost and what the return on your investment will be. Exhibit 6.1 will help you design your customized program while estimating the related costs and considering the factors impinging upon them.

Question 1 focuses on goals, objectives, and missions (see chapter 1). To be successful, the goals and objectives for your proposed grants coaching program must support your institution's/organization's mission(s).

Question 2 deals with clarifying how your grants coaching program will be evaluated. What will change and how much change will be required to meet the goals and objectives of the program? The change should be measurable and a minimum, acceptable amount of change should be identified. Ultimately, this question alludes to how you will determine your institution's/organization's return on its investment. (Chapter 20 focuses on evaluating and improving your grants coaching program.)

In question 3 you are asked to estimate the number of participants/coachees that will be in your grants coaching program. If there are going to be different subgroups within your target population, you will need to estimate the number of participants proposed for each subgroup.

Question 4 requires you to clearly define the target population. Who will be the participants/coachees? Who is the program specifically designed to impact (see chapter 3)? Are there subgroups within the target population?

Question 5 deals with incentives. Many programs provide incentives by subgroups. For example, professors or faculty members get X while professional staff get Y. Identify all of the incentives and the estimated cost for each. Do not forget to consider the costs associated with reassigned time, reduced teaching loads or other duties, stipends, summer support, and travel.

After reviewing the exhibits included in chapters 4 and 5, use this worksheet to help tailor your grants coaching program to your institution/organization and to estimate its cost and potential return on investment.

1. What is the mission(s) of your institution/organization?

   What are the the goals and objectives of your proposed grants coaching program? How will these goals and objectives further the mission(s) of your institution/organization?

2. How will the grants coaching program be evaluated to determine whether the stated goals and objectives have been attained?

   What measurement indicators will be used and what level of change will be acceptable?

3. What is the estimated number of program participants/coachees?

4. Who makes up the target population that will benefit from your program (non-tenured faculty, professional staff, graduate students, etc.)?

   Of the entire target population, what percentage will be from each subgroup?

5. What incentives will be used with the target population and/or with the subgroups within the target population?

   For each incentive, try to calculate the cost per participant/coachee. Multiply this cost by the number of participants to come up with a total cost per incentive. For example:

Incentive	Cost Per Coachee	# of Coachees	Total Cost
Re-assigned or released time			
Stipends			
Special Bonuses			
Travel Funds			
Other			

Exhibit 6.1 Developing Your Grants Coaching Program and Estimating Costs.

6. How long will the grants coaching program last?

   Will more than one grants coaching program be conducted at the same time? If so, how many?

7. What seminars will be included in the program? How long will each be? Estimate instructor fees, room and av equipment costs, refreshment/lunch costs, etc.

Seminar Topic	Instructor Fee	Room/AV Costs	Refreshment/ Lunch Costs	Other Expenses
Government				
Foundation & Corporate				
Team Building				
Quality Circles				
Other:				

8. Specify the materials that will be included for each participant/coachee and estimate the associated costs.

Material	Cost per Item per Coachee	# of Coachees	Total Cost
How To Grants Manual			
Other Book(s)			
Team Dimension Profile (Team Building Seminar)			
Handouts (and/or Reproduction)			
Software			

Exhibit 6.1 (*continued*)

9. Specify the follow-up services that will be included in the program and estimate the associated costs.

Most of the grants coaching program I facilitate include 60-minute, 1-on-1 meetings per coachee every 90 days. For a 1 and ½ year program, I meet with each coachee 5 times. For every 1 day of meetings, I can meet with approximately 8 coachees. Therefore, if my program has 16 participants, every 90 days I conduct 2 days of 1-on-1 meetings for a contract total of ten 10, 1-on-1 meeting days.

Follow-Up Service	Cost of 1 day of 1-on-1 Meetings (Consultant Fee)	# Of 1-on-1 Meetings Days Per Contract	Total Cost (Consultant Fee)
1-on-1 meetings			

The programs I facilitate also include email/phone/skype consultation. Most of my program sponsors budget 1 hour of email/phone/skype follow-up per program participant every 90 days. Assuming my contract is 18-months long, the total contract includes 5 hours of email/phone/skype consultation per coachee. To calculate the total number of hours, I simply multiply the number of coachees by 5.

Follow-Up Service	Cost Per Hour (Consultant Fee)	Total Number of Contracted Hours	Total Cost (Consultant Fee)
Email/Phone/Skype Consultation			
Other			

Exhibit 6.1 (*continued*)

You will also need to consider the costs associated with "special" benefits promised to the participants/coachees for taking part in the program. For example, one program provided participants/coachees access to a small seminar room to meet with other program participants to discuss their problems and progress. Then, when the program participants/coachees expressed a need for assistance in writing up their research results and developing them into published articles, time was established to convene in their designated seminar room and to meet with a hired writing consultant. In this instance, the sponsor incurred some expenses not originally budgeted for, such as room costs and specialty consultant fees.

List the incentives and their associated costs provided per person under question 5 and then multiply the per-person cost by the number of participants. Do not be overwhelmed by your estimated costs. Remember, these costs are associated with your ideal or dream program. If your ideal program is cost prohibitive, you can adjust the incentives offered. While some very effective grants coaching programs have been generous with incentives, other effective programs have offered few incentives other than inclusion in the program.

Question 6 calls for specifying the duration of your grants coaching program. Most programs I have facilitated have been for one to two years. However, some sponsors have overlapping program cohorts. For example, the University of Alabama's program lasts for fifteen months, but a new cohort is started every January. This means two cohort groups are run simultaneously for three months (January, February, and March). On the other hand, programs for "special" populations (like graduate students) and programs focused on preparing proposals for a specific grant (like National Science Foundation Career Awards) may only be eight to ten months in duration. When developing your program, take into consideration that in most instances the longer the program, the more services provided and, hence, the higher the costs.

Question 7 provides for estimating the costs of each seminar offered through your grants coaching program. The main cost to consider is the instructor's fee required by the consultant presenting the seminar and his or her travel expenses. The instructor's fee will probably vary depending on the length of the seminar. For example, what a consultant charges for presenting a half-day seminar will be less than what he or she charges for a whole-day seminar. This does not mean that you should necessarily shorten the length of the seminars included in your program just to cut costs. You must decide what you would like covered in each of the seminars and then how in depth you would like the presentations to be.

What you must come to grips with is the amount of content the consultant can realistically cover in your designated time frames. Chapter 5 provides a curriculum outline for the four suggested seminars—a one-day government grants seminar (exhibit 5.1), a one-day foundation and corporate grants seminar (exhibit 5.2), a half-day team-building seminar (exhibit 5.3), and a half-day quality circle seminar (exhibit 5.4).

You may decide to lengthen the duration of some of your seminars so that you can include special training above and beyond the normal seminar content. For example, in several of my grants coaching programs I took the entire group of participants/coachees to a computer lab and had them all access the grants searching system used by their institution. This activity took some time and had to be squeezed into an already content-packed one-day seminar. You may choose to offer some specialty training like this and either include it in your one-day curriculum or even offer it as a separate training seminar. In either case, expenses related to use of the computer lab must be included in your cost estimates. In addition, when calculating seminar expenses, do not forget costs related to refreshments, lunches, room rentals, and audiovisual equipment.

Question 8 deals with estimating the cost of the materials that will be used in the seminars and in the one-on-one consulting sessions. List the books, software, and other materials that will need to be purchased and identify who will be required to pay for these materials. In my grants coaching programs the sponsors are required to purchase *The "How To" Grants Manual* for each participant/coachee and a self-discovery tool known as the *Team Dimension Profile* for use in my team-building seminar. I provide the seminar handouts and other ancillary materials like project planners and self-learning contracts to the sponsors at no additional cost. However, the sponsors do incur the cost of having the handouts reproduced for each participant.

Question 9 asks you to define the specific aspects of the follow-up services to be included in your program. For example, how will the follow-up one-on-one meetings/interviews be structured? Will the coach be available for e-mail and/or phone consultation that includes reviewing drafts of proposals and answering questions concerning the implementation of proactive strategies such as preproposal contact with grantors? Will the grants coach be asked to access Skype or similar means to assist the program participants/coachees?

List the follow-up services your program will include. Then determine a set number of hours each participant/coachee will be allowed for each activity. By clearly defining these aspects of your program and documenting the time dedicated to these services, you will be able to determine the costs associated with having a grants coach consultant provide these services. If you are thinking of using someone in house as your grants coach, you still need to specify exactly what it is you want to provide in this areas so that you can develop an appropriate job description for your institution's/organization's employee.

The institution/organization that chooses to use an in-house employee as its grants coach must factor into his or her full-time job description the time required to conduct the program. Grants coaching cannot just be added on to an existing full-time job description. It is much too time consuming for that. In addition, teaching the selected seminars and conducting the follow-up coaching activities take considerable dedication. At the very least, you must document the time required to facilitate all aspects of the grants coaching program and then determine the portion of the employee's current job that must be relieved.

The same is true for the grants coaching consultant. The organization that contracts for consultant services must understand the time commitment that is involved in the total grants coaching experience. As a consultant, I have developed a fee based upon the knowledge, skills, and energy needed to provide large group-learning experiences (seminars) as well as what it takes to effectively do one-on-one coaching and other follow-up activities.

One of the critical components of all of the grants coaching programs I have facilitated is individual access to the coach as needed by the coachee. You, as the sponsoring institution/organization, must understand and budget for the fact that all instruction does not happen in the seminars or during the one-on-one meetings. Planning and accounting for this "other" time is difficult, particularly when the external consultant model is used.

My grants coaching contracts include e-mail/phone consultation on grants strategy and the review and critique of draft and final proposals. My sponsors normally base their cost on one hour of follow-up services per program participant/coachee every ninety days of the contract. A typical contract for twenty coachees would equal twenty hours of my time every ninety days. Charged at $150.00 per hour, this amounts to a cost of $3,040 for follow-up services every ninety days. Your cost would obviously be based on what your organization can negotiate with the consultant hired to facilitate your program.

I suggest you take into consideration all of the services you would like to have provided by the coach consultant and then come up with an all-inclusive contract amount. The best way to do this is to calculate the consultant's fee for each of your program's components. For example, negotiate specific consulting fees for:

- one-day seminars;
- half-day seminars;
- each full day of one-on-one meetings; and
- a predesignated amount of follow-up services.

In addition, do not forget to budget for the travel expenses that will be incurred by the consultant. Predetermine what travel expenses will be allowable, how the consultant will be required to document them, and how they will be reimbursed.

Even though the contract will specify the amount for the entire program, reimbursement can be made incrementally, after each component is completed. This way your organization/institution will not find itself in the difficult position of trying to pay for services before they are delivered.

As an alternative, you can hire a consultant who uses a retainer from which his or her direct services are then billed. While this method may work well in the legal field, I have found retainers a difficult way to pay for consulting activities. For one thing, the retainer has to be put aside in full by the sponsoring organization prior to the delivery of services. Second, the sponsoring organization/institution must rely on the consultant to accurately record the amount of time spent on delivering the contracted services and billing correctly.

So, how much should it cost to conduct a grants coaching program? You can now see the cost of your program is based on many factors including:

- the duration of your program;
- the number of program participants;
- the incentives, educational components (i.e., seminars, one-on-one meetings), materials, and follow-up services you choose to include;
- whether the program is conducted by an employee of your organization/institution or a consultant; and
- if applicable, the fees charged by the consultant for the desired services and travel.

Remember, you have the power to control your grants coaching program costs by designing it to include only those components that your institution/organization can afford and those that are likely to secure the desired return on investment.

Part II

THE GRANTS COACH

Chapter Seven

Grants Coaching Basics

I have served as a grants coach for several years and have facilitated grants coaching programs at a number of institutions. Based on post-program statistics compiled by research administrators at these universities, I feel confident in saying that overall my coachees have experienced 50–60 percent grants success rates since completing their programs. However, since each institution's grants coaching program included measurement indicators unique to its particular program, it is difficult to compare one program's success with another. But, in terms of basic structure, the similarities within the programs illuminate the essential elements of a successful grants coaching program.

As you begin your exploration into grants coaching, read *The "How To" Grants Manual*. This manual has evolved over the last thirty years and is currently in its eighth edition. While it contains many concepts that you may decide to incorporate into your coaching, it is more than just a compilation of successful grant-seeking strategies. It contains lots of other information you will need as a grants coach.

For example, it looks at how to develop career plans, how to build consortia and teams, and how to help grant seekers employ time management techniques so they can incorporate proactive grants strategies into their daily work schedules. The *"How To" Grants Manual* allocates much time to clarifying career goals, developing very specific one-year grants plans, creating less specific five-year plans, and learning how to assimilate grant-seeking strategies into career plans. My grants coaching mirrors the information presented in *The "How To" Grants Manual*, and, who knows, perhaps yours will too!

THE GRANTS COACHING STRUCTURE

Even though coaching skills differ from one field to another (i.e., sports coaching, financial coaching, and so on), some coaching concepts are common irrespective of the area. Successful coaches have knowledge, experience, and a track record of success in their field. In addition, they have employed many strategies over the course of their careers and have fine-tuned those approaches they believe will result in success for those they coach. For example, as a grants coach, one of the things you will be expected to do is use your expertise and skills in grants training and consulting to provide a learning experience that results in coachees who master the grant-seeking process.

Coaching implies that the coach will help the coachee learn, practice, and develop the expertise needed to succeed. The coach does not play the game. The coachees play the game under the coach's tutelage, direction, and prompting. In personal fitness training, the level of adherence to a training regime increases as the coach assists in motivating the coachee to stick to his or her plan. The same concept can be applied to grants coaching. The likelihood of my coachees meeting their program's benchmarks goes up dramatically when I e-mail them to remind them of our upcoming face-to-face meeting and the proactive grant-seeking steps they agreed to accomplish prior to our meeting.

The following is a list of the primary activities provided by a grants coach. They are also the basis for the subsequent chapters of this book.

The grants coach will:

- provide training sessions or seminars to expose coachees to the basic constructs that support the ultimate grant-winning strategy;
- offer individualized training that may include the use of CDs, DVDs, or other tools to develop the coachees' knowledge of the grants field;
- present training on the use of computer searching systems and grants databases to develop the coachees' ability to locate prospective grantors after the grants coaching experience concludes;
- deliver training and individual instruction in developing a plan that includes successful grant-seeking strategies and assistance in the implementation of funded grants;
- identify which of the coachees' existing skills can be applied to winning grants;
- assist coachees in developing new skills necessary to succeed, such as how to find and choose advisors and co-principal investigators; and
- develop the most efficient strategies to keep each coachee on his or her consistent plan for grants success.

One interesting notion shared by many coaches is that they do not *teach* the skills necessary for success in their fields. They believe that the skills are already in their coachees and that their job is to get them to recognize these skills and to understand when and how to employ them.

As discussed in the introduction, grants coaching is not just training, consulting, or mentoring. It is all of these, and more. While grants coaching embodies many facets, the coach's overall approach is what defines the program. For instance, my grants coaching involves asking my coachees inductive questions, listening to them, and getting them to express their own knowledge when developing their unique plans. My coaching does not include much directive instruction or mentoring (i.e., do as I say). I practice more of an inductive approach. For example, a mentor might say, "I do it this way and you should too." Whereas my grants coaching focuses on the coachee, how a certain successful grant strategy could be adapted to his or her plans, and how he or she feels about it. I believe that through my grants coaching approach the coachee's plans, aspirations, and personality come together to form a valuable life experience.

One of the basic constructs I employ in grants coaching is to tell coachees that this may be the first time in their lives that a program for self-improvement focuses totally on them. I help to make them aware of the fact that seldom in their educational experience has the attainment of their goals been the basis for a program. I remind them that the program is truly all about them, their careers, and how successful grant seeking will enhance their personal goals and objectives. I also let them know that grants coaching is the most rewarding educational tool I have ever employed because of its potential, positive impact on the careers of others.

Chapter Eight

The Role of the Grants Coach

I have been a teacher/educator for forty-five years and have instructed over forty thousand grant seminar participants. Approximately 80 percent of those participants completed an evaluation of their learning experience. The feedback I have received on their learning experience has been a crucial ingredient in changing my teaching techniques and in developing new materials and exercises for large and small group instruction.

I do not believe that individuals are born teachers. What I do believe is that individuals can become more effective or successful teachers by gathering feedback from their students and adapting and changing their behaviors, methods, and strategies accordingly. Successful teachers continually evaluate their effectiveness. For example, I frequently question the effectiveness of the proactive grant-seeking system I have developed and, in particular, if and how the proactive grant-seeking strategies I profess impact the success rates of my seminar participants and coachees. Then I make adjustments to my system accordingly.

Questioning the effectiveness of my teaching stems from the fact that my first college degree was not in education. It was in psychology. It was in that course of study that I learned to question the degree to which I was effective in improving an existing situation/environment. My work in industrial psychology helped me to develop an appreciation for how complex changing a person's behavior can be even when the potential outcome is great.

I consider myself fortunate to have evolved into teaching from the field of psychology because I never learned how to teach or went out to practice teach. I was instead dropped into a classroom to teach inner-city minority youth to develop healthy behaviors in the midst of drug/alcohol abuse, sexually transmitted diseases, and teen pregnancy. I taught them the correct health concepts, and most of them passed my knowledge-based tests with flying colors.

Unfortunately, their unhealthy behaviors did not change and the problems they faced grew larger. Then, as New York State's 1970 Health Educator of the Year, I was asked to evaluate over $20 million in health-related federal, state, foundation, and corporate grants. That is when I really learned that changing behaviors by teaching facts did not actually lead to the desired healthy outcomes.

In grants coaching we seek to increase the coachees' grants marketplace knowledge. However, as with health education, simply learning the facts is not enough. You need to make sure that your coachees also change their existing "bad" grant-seeking habits and learn how to use their expanded grants knowledge to adopt more positive, effective grant-seeking strategies and behaviors that reflect that knowledge. It is the coach's responsibility to make sure that his or her coachees accept the fact that positive and valuable outcomes often require change and that change can be scary and threatening. You can add to your skill in this area by reading *Change Anything: The New Science of Personal Success*.[1] You will find the strategies in this book helpful when trying to get your coachees to change their grant-seeking behaviors. In addition, the skills taught in this book may also help you change your behavior from consultant/expert to coach.

As you now know, your primary goal as a grants coach is to create a learning atmosphere that will ultimately be responsible for the success of your coachees. However, how you blend the tasks of teacher/educator, reflective listener, change agent, and mentor into one definable role will be instrumental to the success of your grants coaching program.

THE GRANTS COACH AS A TEACHER/EDUCATOR

As a health educator encouraging teenagers to make healthy decisions, I developed proposals that resulted in millions of dollars in grants. Along the way, I made many mistakes, but I worked hard on improving my success rate and reducing the time wasted on writing proposals that were destined to be rejected. My colleagues asked me to help them become more successful in grant seeking, and as I did, I wrote my first book on the subject and started teaching seminars on the broader aspects of grant seeking. Eventually, results from the evaluations of thousands of my grants seminar participants drove me to embrace the concept of grants coaching and the support and follow-up activities that have proven to be the game changer in my coachees' adoption of a successful, proactive grant-seeking system.

The grants coach as a teacher/educator is the best way to transfer the facts on effective grants strategies. The traditional didactic lecture approach gets the basic proactive steps across in a cost-effective manner. By starting with the group instruction approach, you can avoid repeating the basic constructs over and over again to each coachee and your individual grants coaching time can be used to help each coachee implement the grants strategies he or she learned in your lectures.

While I suggest large group lecture instruction to lay out the basic constructs of grants success, this teacher-focused technique can be boring and tedious for the participants. Therefore, it is a good idea to incorporate small group exercises/activities within the lecture format to consolidate and augment the concepts. This will encourage the coachees to practice and apply the concepts with fellow coachees and your training class or seminar will be considered interesting.

For example, a lecture/didactic explanation of the importance of focusing on the problem/need statement in a proposal *before* presenting the solution can be emphasized by conducting the following small group activity: Ask each coachee to describe the problem his or her proposal will address in five sentences without mentioning the solution. Then ask the coachee to share his or her problem/need statement with a partner. Encourage your coachees to discuss ways to improve their statements with their partners and to brainstorm ways to make them clearer and more critical or urgent to address.

My coaching program uses large group seminars to build my coachees' knowledge base. Chapter 5 outlines the four teaching/lecture seminars that I include in my grants coaching programs—Federal/Government Grants, Foundation/Corporate Grants, Team/Consortium Building, and Quality Circles/Mock Reviews. The curriculum for these seminars is based on the content in *The "How To" Grants Manual* and on the scope and sequence of the steps I have found work best in developing and practicing successful, proactive grant seeking.

THE GRANTS COACH AS A REFLECTIVE LISTENER

Coachees need to feel that their coach hears them and attends to their particular needs. To create an atmosphere of trust and openness, I assure coachees that their conversations with me are confidential and will not be shared with anyone without their permission. Since my first individual coaching session begins with a discussion on the coachee's vision of success in his or her field, conversation usually flows easily. I simply encourage the coachee to talk about him or herself and listen. I also often ask questions in this session to get the coachee to open up even more. For example, I might ask how the coachee's vision of success in his or her field has changed over the years, or who has been influential in his or her development.

Subsequent one-on-one meetings can be more difficult since they often involve reviewing activities that the coachee said he or she would undertake but did not. In these cases, the conversation does not flow as effortlessly. I realize that it would be easier for me if I just told the coachee what his or her best choice was or what the best grants behavior would be in a particular situation. However, I have to remind myself that coachees need to figure it out for themselves. This is best accomplished by asking inductive questions. It is much more open and conversation inducing to ask "How do you feel about these goals?" than to comment on how you see them. Again, it is critical that you encourage the coachees to talk about themselves and to listen.

I was fortunate enough to have had Dr. Carl Rodgers, the father of reflective listening, as a professor. The concept he professed is quite simple and can easily be applied to grants coaching. By reflecting back to the coachee what he or she has said to you, your coachee will most likely elaborate on his or her comments. When you feel it is appropriate, you can ask questions that induce the coachee to explain even more. To accomplish this, avoid asking questions that can be responded to with a yes or no. Grants coaching involves listening to your coachees and developing a trust that enables your coachees to realize you are there to help them reach their goals through grant-funded projects.

If you are a grants consultant who wants to add grants coaching to your skill set and to market a grants coaching program to your clients, it is essential that you learn how to ask inductive questions and practice reflective listening. These may be two of the hardest behaviors to adopt and assimilate into your work style.

As a grants consultant I found that few of my clients wanted me to be a reflective listener or to ask inductive questions. Grants consultants are generally on the spot to provide answers, knowledge, and expertise, and not to respond with, "That's an intriguing question. What do you think?" The role of a grants coach changes the situation from what you think as a grants consultant expert to let us explore what grant-seeking strategies may be best for you and how you feel about implementing them.

In addition, the business model for many grants consultants is often quite different than that of the grants coach. The consultant business model operates under the premise that the consultant is the expert and that his or her clients will always need him or her to tell them what to do and how to do it. Unlike consultants, grants coaches operate under the premise that they eventually will not be there for their coachees. Hence, their goal is for the coachees to learn what to do and to be able to deduce the correct action for themselves in their future grants quests. Indeed, the role of the grants coach is to develop in the coachee the ability to solve the problem, choose the best grant strategy, and to not need the coach any more. The grants coach must teach, lead, listen, and use his or her skills to teach coachees to fish without fishing for them.

I have to admit that as a grants consultant even I did not always employ this concept. I had to work hard on adopting the appropriate practices to succeed in grants coaching and you may have to also. In fact, some grants consultants who want to move to grants coaching will have great difficulty assuming the role of grants coach.

What I have discovered is a bit of a compromise from the autocratic response of "Just do this." Instead I now ask, "From what you learned in the seminar, what could you apply to figure out your particular situation/problem?" The goal of instilling in your coachees the confidence to arrive at solutions on their own is best embraced by the philosophy of Socratic learning. The truly great teacher asks the right question at the perfect time so that the learner can figure out the answers for him or herself and own them.

This reminds me of a situation I had with one of my coachees. She complained bitterly that the research fellowship program I was facilitating required that each participant make a visit to the appropriate federal program officer. This fellow even e-mailed the president of the university to complain about this requisite. When all was said and done, she was still required to make the visit.

She reluctantly went to meet with who she thought was the appropriate officer. This person promptly escorted her down the hall to his colleague who was the appropriate official and who was delighted with her idea. She returned and insisted that my new group of fellows heed *her* advice and make contact with program officers. It was now *her* idea to make contact. It is truly an educator's dream when a concept and behavior become the learner's instead of the teacher's.

THE GRANTS COACH AS A MENTOR

As you consider incorporating mentor skills into the grants coaching experience, it is useful to contrast the role of a mentor versus coach. The term "mentoring" is attributed to Homer's classic work, *The Odyssey*. When Odysseus left his son to go to the Trojan War, he asked his friend Mentor to act as a tutor for his son.[2] A tutor and a mentor generally analyze and provide critical comments based upon their past experiences. It is more of a "do as I say" relationship rather than a coaching connection. In fact, it may be useful to enlist a separate mentor for certain grant-related components such as post-award activities. Post-award and practices governing project implementation and completion may best be transferred in the "do as I have done" learning technique. Since grant fulfillment and completion involves many government circulars and rules, a mentor's experience seems appropriate.

Grants coaches may at times mentor but the atmosphere of correction and critiquing that is affiliated with mentoring is not conducive to the overall coaching atmosphere of encouragement and self-discovery. Yet multiple studies have found that having "a formal mentor is highly correlated with research productivity (Blackburn, 1979; Bland and Schmitz, 1986; Cameron and Blackburn, 1981; Corcoran and Clark, 1984; Mills, 1995; Mundt, 2001). . . . With regard to faculty success, Rogers, Holloway, and Miller (1990) define mentorship as the 'influence, guidance, or direction exerted by a close, trusted, and experienced counselor. A mentor is to be detached and disinterested to some degree, so that he or she can hold up a mirror for the protégé.'"[3]

In their book, *The Research-Productive Department*, Bland, Weber-Main, Lund, and Finstad do an excellent search of the literature on mentoring faculty. They quote five more recent studies that validate mentoring with researchers. However, they do caution in their book that the process and components of mentoring programs differ from one to another and that they are not equally successful or replicable.

The point of this for you, the grants coach, is that you need to encourage your coachees to locate one or two successful researchers in his or her field to develop a relationship based on common research goals. It may begin with the formation of an advisory group that the coachee can trust to share research ideas and protocols with and grow to a Co-PI relationship.

Many coachees come into my programs with a university- or department-assigned mentor. These mentors are usually more senior faculty with experience and some success in grant seeking. While the mentor will probably have more expertise in his or her research specialty, he or she may never have actually practiced proactive grant seeking.

At one of my programs, all sixteen of my coachees had preassigned mentors. The mentors consisted of the old guard who sat on tenure committees. My coachees were instructed by many of these senior faculty members to write and submit as many proposals as possible each year since they knew that the tenure committee took into consideration how many proposals were submitted and for what amount of money, irrespective of what was actually awarded. Some of the coachees were producing eight to ten NSF proposals each year. However, none of them were funded.

When I insisted that my coachees select only two or three of their grant applications and apply my proactive steps to their grant seeking, they objected and their mentors supported their dissention. I cancelled my program because I knew that in that particular research atmosphere I could not help my coachees succeed. Based on this experience, I strongly suggest that if your client has a mentoring program, invite the mentors to at least the first hour of your initial presentation/session to ascertain that they will buy into your grants coaching program. In fact, you should invite them to all of your large group presentations but particularly the quality circle seminar and the mock review of their mentee's proposal. Once they take part in these activities they will understand how quality circles can be instrumental in improving proposals and increasing success rates. This will help get the quality circle concept endorsed and even used by some faculty.

If the target population of your grants coaching program is graduate students rather than faculty members, it is beneficial to incorporate your students' advisors into the program by inviting them to your grants seminar or at least the first one that focuses on developing career grants plans as part of the federal grants seminar. Normally, these advisors act as mentors because of their expertise in specific content areas. I instruct graduate students that there are two major ways to locate funding to pay for the graduate education and that both require the involvement of their advisors.

The first way is to locate a grant specifically for dissertations, fellowships, scholarships, and so on. Websites like GraduateStudents.com can help them in this endeavor. However, even when they locate a potential funding source, the grantor will usually require the student's advisor/mentor to endorse his or her application and the research that will be the proposal's focus.

The other major way to secure grant funding is for the graduate student to locate funding for his or her advisor's research that includes support for a graduate student. While graduate students may locate many grant sources interested in their research, applicants may be restricted to only those with a terminal degree. With your help, your graduate student coachees may be able to locate funding for grants in which their mentors are the principal investigators and they are included in supportive roles and paid for their time.

In my program for graduate students at the University of North Carolina Greensboro, the advisors/mentors are encouraged to attend any or all of program's seminars, but especially the quality circle/mock review workshop. This is because the proposals critiqued at this workshop often mirror the research/projects that will ultimately be approved by the graduate students' advisors/mentors and dissertation committee members.

When it comes to the grants coach as a mentor, just remember this. The grants coach may use some of the techniques that a subject-expert mentor uses to set a good example. But the grants coach is not truly a mentor. He or she just selects to use certain mentor techniques when appropriate.

THE GRANTS COACH AS A CHANGE AGENT

The ability to instruct on successful grant-winning techniques resides in or emanates from the coach. The motivation to successfully carry out the techniques resides in or emanates from the coachee. The coach locates those forces that exist in the coachee that will propel him or her to success and focuses on them. The coach encourages the coachee to employ the appropriate techniques and provides incentives when they are implemented. I remind my coachees that I cannot motivate them and that they must motivate themselves. Motivation comes from them. However, as their coach, I help them realize the desired state of affairs that will be attained when they obtain their grant award. In reality, I am not a motivator but rather an agent of change.

As mentioned in the introduction, my coachees must use a self-learning contract that they create with me and sign to guide their grant-seeking behavior for the next thirty, sixty, and ninety days. This assists in their motivation. The coachees do not want to sit face-to-face with me and report that they did not accomplish the tasks they wrote down on their contracts to achieve their grants success. They were motivated because they:

- did not want to admit they had failed to do what they agreed to;
- feared they would disappoint me, their coach;
- worried that a bad report might eliminate them from the program; and
- wanted to keep the incentive funding included in their grants coaching program.

No matter what the coachees' reasons are for finishing the tasks on their contracts, they are responsible for making the time to complete them. As their coach, I remind them by e-mail, phone, and Skype that *they* place the items on their contract and only *they* are responsible for *their* completion. Of course, everyday life can create cause for change. As their coach, I am flexible and remember that it is their careers and not mine. The coachee may have to make changes and move items to a later date. I remind them of the reality we work under. If the grants coaching program has milestones and performance criteria they agreed to when joining the program, I ask them how they plan to rearrange their schedules to allow for completion.

Some coachees have had to drop out of their grants coaching programs and rejoin the next one offered after the life event has been dealt with. In my ten-plus years of running grants coaching programs I have never had to eject any coachees. But on occasion, the threat of expulsion from the program and the stress of additional responsibilities like grant seeking have resulted in voluntary resignations. I may have been a catalyst in these resignations in that I did help these few faculty members realize that their jobs were not for them and that they had not fully considered the rigors of teaching, grant seeking, and publishing. But, all in all, I feel that these former coachees made the best decision for themselves and their careers.

As a coach I am often amazed at how much my coachees take on. But their motivation and their capacity to integrate grant seeking with their other work is their business.

When they are awarded the grant and when they attend the program graduation, they often report that I motivated them. My response is always the same: I remind them that I cannot and did not motivate them. They motivated themselves. I was merely the catalyst in helping them get funded faster than they would have if they took a trial-and-error path to grants success. The fact of the matter is that these successful coachees probably put off some of life's more pleasurable activities and deferred their gratification to get their proposals completed in a proactive and timely manner. They get all the credit.

I hope you can now differentiate between the many roles of the grants coach and know when to apply each of them while continually maintaining a cooperative, trusting relationship with your coachees that ultimately results in grants success.

EVALUATING AND IMPROVING THE GRANT COACH'S EFFECTIVENESS

Your role as a grants coach includes being a teacher, listener, mentor, and change agent. Since all of these functions are critical for the success of your grants coaching program, you need to know how well your coachees feel you are accomplishing each of these components and what behaviors may be keeping you from achieving the effectiveness you desire. As with each part of the grants coaching process, feedback is the key ingredient for improvement and change. Evaluation and feedback will be encouraged in each area of the grants coaching process. The role and attitude of the coach have a pervasive influence on the ultimate success of the coachee integrating the positive grants behaviors and on the success of the coaching program.

One of the most effective techniques I have discovered for obtaining feedback is to video-record the coachees' one-on-one sessions. (You do not need to video-record all of the sessions. But it is a good idea to do intermittently.) You will need to obtain permission from the coachee to record the session and explain what the video recording will be used for. You will need to assure him or her that it is to analyze your performance, that no one but you will see it without his or her prior approval, and that it will be erased after it is reviewed. As always, the experience is all about them and their grant success. All you are doing is trying to obtain insight into how you can improve your role as their grants coach.

Exhibit 8.1 can be used to help you analyze your session. If you want to further validate your evaluation, you can ask a colleague to review it to be certain you have made the proper conclusions. Remember, however, that if anyone else is to review the recording, you will need to get prior permission from the coachee.

Review the recorded session. Start and stop each time you want to examine what you are both saying and doing. Make note of your body language and the coachee's. Stop the recording at one-minute intervals and check the response boxes in exhibit 8.1 that represent your behavior or write in a response if none of the listed ones are appropriate. Analyze the results by adding up the responses and comparing them to your learning objectives for that session with that particular coachee.

Name of Coachee: _____
Date of Video Session: _____
Objective of the Session: _____
Based on Your Review of the Video:
1. What percent of the time did you, the coach, talk? _____ What percent of the time did the coachee talk? _____
2. How many times did you, the coach, ask inductive questions, ask for the clarification of details, and/or request more information? _____ _____
3. What percent of the time was devoted to reporting on how successful the coachee was in completing the prescribed tasks on his or her contract? _____
4. What percent of time was used to explore what was learned from past tasks and how this newly acquired knowledge may be used to help complete the tasks on the coachee's next 90 day contract? (Note: The number of days between contracts can be adjusted to reflect your particular grants coaching program. It does not have to be 90.) _____
5. How many suggestions did you provide the coachee on how he or she could improve his or her grants success strategy? _____
6. Were there any other areas worth noting from the video? Is so, please explain. _____ _____ _____ _____

Exhibit 8.1 Coach's Evaluation of Video-Recorded Session.

Your role changes by the objectives you specify for each meeting. For example, a coachee that is not accomplishing his or her tasks may be asked an inductive question like what is holding them back or what could be a helping force in keeping them on track. Depending on the coachee's responses and where you, the coach, can help develop some action plans, you may move to a more autocratic leadership style and suggest strategies for the coachee to employ.

Periodically through the grants coaching process ask your coachees to complete exhibit 8.2 (or your own tailored version of it) to help you improve your role. Completion of exhibit 8.2 will provide you with valuable feedback on how your role, attitude, and behaviors are perceived by the coachees. Acknowledge that their responses are designed to improve your performance and the effectiveness of your work together to achieve grants success. Keep the ultimate goal clearly in mind. It is not whether the coachees like you. It is whether they recognize and accept your ability to help them develop the proactive behaviors that lead to funding.

Using a scale of 1 to 5 with 1 being "needs improvement", 2 being "fair", 3 being "good", 4 being "very good", and 5 being "excellent", please rate your grants coach in the following areas:

Displays a sincere concern for my grants success	1	2	3	4	5
Listens to me and my grant related concerns	1	2	3	4	5
Understands the pressures of my job and helps me integrate time management and proactive grant strategies into my work	1	2	3	4	5
Suggests alternative strategies when I confront problems	1	2	3	4	5
Keeps me positive and upbeat even when I encounter setbacks and rejection	1	2	3	4	5
Exhibits a realistic and current knowledge of the grants marketplace	1	2	3	4	5
Responds promptly to my email and phone requests for assistance	1	2	3	4	5

Exhibit 8.2   Coachee's Evaluation/Feedback Form.

NOTES

1. Kerry Patterson, Joseph Grenny, David Maxfield, Ron McMillan, and Al Switzler, *Change Anything: The New Science of Personal Success* (New York: Business Plus Hachette Book Group, 2011).

2. Carole J. Bland, Anne Marie Weber-Main, Sharon Marie Lund, and Deborah A. Finstad, *The Research-Productive Department* (p. 64) (Bolton, MA: Anker, 2005).

3. Carole J. Bland, Anne Marie Weber-Main, Sharon Marie Lund, and Deborah A. Finstad, *The Research-Productive Department* (p. 65) (Bolton, MA: Anker, 2005).

Chapter Nine

Helping Coachees Develop Their Career Grants/Research Plans

The "How To" Grants Manual provides the detailed steps critical to achieving grants success. The free downloadable exhibits in the book provide a step-by-step curriculum that has proven to be highly successful. The process has been evaluated by hundreds of my coachees.

The purpose of this book is not to present what is already in *The "How To" Grants Manual* but to provide the grants coach with insights and additional strategies to use with his or her coachees. I suggest reading chapter 8 of the *"How To"* entitled "Your Plan for Success and How to Get There." It seems inconceivable that of the thousands of participants in my past seminars, 90 percent did not have a plan for how to integrate grant seeking into their career plans. In addition, only a few had a vision of success to guide their careers and the professional decisions they must make. More importantly, of those with a vision of success not one seemed to understand the role that grant funding could play in attaining success as they defined it.

Most self-improvement and motivation programs profess that a clear vision is critical to attain success. Therefore, one of your responsibilities as a grants coach is to help your coachees understand that their vision of success provides a rudder for their ship. Without a vision, any grant looks good. But unfortunately, some grants could actually move them off course and away from their ultimate goals. Attaining their goals should be their internal motivator for defining their vision. Coachees who know where they are going focus on what will get them there. They defer gratification of a more temporal nature to gain a greater good through achievement of a longer-term goal that is secured through successful grant seeking.

I require my coachees to complete exhibit 9.1 to help them determine their personal vision and what role grant seeking will play in that vision. Knowing that they need a vision of success in order to develop their one- to five-year plans, I have them work on this exhibit right at the beginning of my grants coaching program. I usually include it as part of the government grants seminar since most of my coachees are required to start their grants quest by seeking federal funding that moves them toward their vision of success while meeting the grantors' needs.

1. Vision
   - What is your vision of success in your field?
   - What part of that vision will you have achieved in five years?
   - What projects, programs, and research will you be performing?
   - How do these projects, programs, and research fit into your vision of success?
   - What part of these will be grant supported?

2. Re-assigned Time – What percent of your time each year will be devoted to these projects/programs/research as opposed to your current job responsibilities?

   Year 1 _____ Year 2 _____ Year 3 _____ Year 4 _____ Year 5 _____

   Based on the percent of time you will be devoting to projects/programs/research, what is the Estimated cost of your grant related salary/wages including fringe benefits each year?

   Year 1 _____ Year 2 _____ Year 3 _____ Year 4 _____ Year 5 _____

3. What personnel will be required to assist you in performing the tasks you would like to accomplish each year of your vision and what is the estimated cost?

   Project Coordinator(s)
   Number: Year 1 _____ Year 2 _____ Year 3 _____ Year 4 _____ Year 5 _____
   Cost: Year 1 _____ Year 2 _____ Year 3 _____ Year 4 _____ Year 5 _____

   Laboratory Assistant(s)
   Number: Year 1 _____ Year 2 _____ Year 3 _____ Year 4 _____ Year 5 _____
   Cost: Year 1 _____ Year 2 _____ Year 3 _____ Year 4 _____ Year 5 _____

   Graduate Assistant(s)
   Number: Year 1 _____ Year 2 _____ Year 3 _____ Year 4 _____ Year 5 _____
   Cost: Year 1 _____ Year 2 _____ Year 3 _____ Year 4 _____ Year 5 _____

   Work Study Student(s)
   Number: Year 1 _____ Year 2 _____ Year 3 _____ Year 4 _____ Year 5 _____
   Cost: Year 1 _____ Year 2 _____ Year 3 _____ Year 4 _____ Year 5 _____

   Other (list):
   Number: Year 1 _____ Year 2 _____ Year 3 _____ Year 4 _____ Year 5 _____
   Cost: Year 1 _____ Year 2 _____ Year 3 _____ Year 4 _____ Year 5 _____

5. What facilities will be required to house these individuals each year? In-house, off-campus, etc. What do you estimate the required square footage to be each year?

	Facility	Square Footage
Year 1:	_____	_____
Year 2:	_____	_____
Year 3:	_____	_____
Year 4:	_____	_____
Year 5:	_____	_____

6. What new equipment (computers, software, machines, vehicles, etc.) will you and your staff need each to accomplish the projected tasks and what will the estimated cost be?

	New Equipment	Estimated Cost
Year 1:	_____	_____

Exhibit 9.1 Your Personal Grants Plan.

Year 2: _____ _____
Year 3: _____ _____
Year 4: _____ _____
Year 5: _____ _____

7. How many articles will you submit each year and to what journals?

	#	Journal
Year 1:	_____	_____
Year 2:	_____	_____
Year 3:	_____	_____
Year 4:	_____	_____
Year 5:	_____	_____

Books or chapters for publication? If yes, how many and under what titles?

	#	Title
Year 1:	_____	_____
Year 2:	_____	_____
Year 3:	_____	_____
Year 4:	_____	_____
Year 5:	_____	_____

8. Attendance, presentation, and or committee participation, at conferences/meetings? If yes, how many and at what conferences/meetings?

	#	Conference/Meeting	Presentation	Committee Participation
Year 1:	_____	_____	_____	_____
Year 2:	_____	_____	_____	_____
Year 3:	_____	_____	_____	_____
Year 4:	_____	_____	_____	_____
Year 5:	_____	_____	_____	_____

9. Based on salary/wages, personnel, and equipment, what is the total amount of resources needed each year? Of this total how much will be requested each year from your organization/institution? How much will be need in grants each year?

	Total	From Organization/Institution	From Grants
Year 1:	_____	_____	_____
Year 2:	_____	_____	_____
Year 3:	_____	_____	_____
Year 4:	_____	_____	_____
Year 5:	_____	_____	_____

Exhibit 9.1 (*continued*)

Question 1 will get your coachees thinking about their vision of success and how grants will be a catalyst in achieving it. Refer back to their vision statement throughout the coaching program to help the coachees develop a rationale for making grant-related decisions. For example, when my coachees fail to achieve tasks on their ninety-day contracts, I ask them if they have changed their vision or if it is no longer important. This usually helps to get them back on track.

I suggest you get them started on question 1 during the first hour of your seminar/program. I divide the coachees into groups of two and request that they share their vision with their partner. This gives them the opportunity to express themselves in less threatening atmosphere than a large group.

To answer this question completely the coachee must articulate his or her lofty goals and prestigious awards. Many coachees feel it is bragging when asked to complete this task. They are embarrassed to say they want to be granted a Fulbright or some other significant award in their field. However, it is important for you to encourage them to broach the subject of awards, recognition by membership groups they belong to, and articles and books they would like to write. Remind them the goal of question 1 is to get them to provide a broad statement of their vision. They can answer the other questions that ask for more detail on their own, outside of the seminar, and bring them to their one-on-one individual consultation meeting.

Ask the coachees to identify what part of the vision they think they will have achieved in five years. Knowing what projects, programs, and research they hope to be performing will prove useful as you work with them to select the best grants to allow them to do those things.

Question 2 forces the coachee to deal with the time it will take to create grant proposals and actually conduct his or her sponsored project. Many beginning grant seekers want their institutions to pay them for this work or release them from their current duties to enable them to create grant proposals. While I have facilitated grants coaching programs at institutions that had very strict labor laws, most did not provide for paid released or reassigned time to create grant proposals. In fact, it is difficult to get an institution to allow the successful grantee to get time off from their normal duties even when the grant is funded.

The point is to get the coachees to begin thinking about the time it will take to perform the activities that are required in their grants. Frequently, professors want to continue to devote some portion of their time to teaching. However, research-driven universities may want the researcher to be conducting research full-time. With all of this in mind, the coachee is asked to project how his or her time commitment to funded grants will change over the course of the five years. Once the estimate of time devoted to research/grants is made, the coachee can then estimate the cost of his or her annual grant-related salary/wages including fringe benefits.

Question 3 asks the coachee to forecast the grant/research-related support staff he/she will need to carry out his/her research. While these numbers will probably be rough estimates, they will still help in calculating the facilities that will be required to house these individuals (see question 4).

Question 4 examines facility and square footage needs.

Question 5 asks the coachee to forecast his/her equipment needs. His or her answer to this question, in conjunction with his/her answers to question 3 (number of support staff) and question 4 (space required to house support staff), provides the coachee with the information necessary to request his/her facility needs before they are actually required. This is helpful to administrators who need to budget or plan ahead for upcoming /future space needs.

Question 6 requires the coachees to be very specific about the number of articles they submit each year and the journals they will submit the articles to for publication. They cannot simply say, "Several articles in quality journals." They have to be explicit. Obviously, their institution or organization will want them to submit to high-quality journals. However, if their articles are rejected, they can then target less prestigious journals.

Question 6 also asks about books or chapters for publication and attendance and/or presentations at conferences/meetings. Once again, the coachees' responses should be as specific as possible.

The coachee's responses to question 6 will be used to calculate the time he or she will realistically have for creating grant proposals.

Question 7 calls for estimating the costs for the total amount of resources needed each year.

By completing exhibit 9.1, your coachee will have a good idea of the activities he or she will be working on over the next five years. Exhibit 9.2 is a sample of a completed five-year personal grants plan. Have your coachee plot his/her first year activities on a timeline. As potential grant programs and their associated deadlines are identified, they should be added to the timeline along with the dates for accomplishing the necessary proactive grant strategies. Plotting activities as well as grant programs and deadlines on timelines could end up being very beneficial. For example, if the coachee has his/her conferences on his/her timeline as well as potential grantors, he or she could contact the grantors to see if they are also planning to attend the conference. If so, the coachee could make an appointment to meet with the grantor at the conference.

When your coachees complete exhibit 9.1 they will realize how little time they really have to accomplish the proactive steps necessary for grants success. This is when it is time for the coach to suggest time management strategies. Review chapter 4 of *The "How To" Grants Manual* to obtain tips and techniques on how your coachees can integrate time management into a successful grants career. You may also want to look at some of the top ten books on time management according to amazon.com (listed on page 38 of *The "How To"*) and Amelia Gray's article, "Top 50 Apps for Time Management" (referenced on page 39 of *The "How To"*).

My coachees have found it very helpful to carve out a set amount of time each week to review their plans and complete the appropriate proactive grant steps. Many of them have found that one hour per week can actually make a tremendous difference. That's fifty-two hours over a year, not fifty-two hours right before the deadline!

1. Vision

What is your vision of success in your field?
- Internationally recognized researcher, name recognition, young graduates wanting to work in my group, to be generally considered an authority in the field
- Achieved via publications, invitations for talks
- Elected fellowship and/or research awards from Electrochemical Society (such as Uhlig Award), International Society of Electrochemistry, American Chemical Society, and Materials Research Society

What part of that vision will you have achieved in five years?
- Should be on the trajectory; at least known in smaller cities
- Widely published
- Premium publications

What projects, programs, and research will you be performing?
- Electrochemical Applications in Materials and Biological research
- Advanced Nuclear Materials
- Microbial Electrochemistry for Environment and Energy

How do these projects, programs, and research fit into your vision of success?
- My interests are directly aligned

What part of these will be grant supported?
- 100% ideally

2. Re-assigned Time – What percent of your time each year will be devoted to these projects/programs/research as opposed to your current job responsibilities?

Year 1 40%   Year 2 40%   Year 3 50%   Year 4 50%   Year 5 60%

Based on the percent of time you will be devoting to projects/programs/research, what is the Estimated cost of your grant related salary/wages including fringe benefits each year?

Year 1 $55K   Year 2 $55K   Year 3 $80K   Year 4 $80K   Year 5 $110K

Exhibit 9.2 Sample Personal Grants Plan.

3. What personnel will be required to assist you in performing the tasks you would like to accomplish each year of your vision and what is the estimated cost?

Graduate Student (GS)/Project Director (PD)
Number: Year 1 <u>4GS</u>   Year 2 <u>5GS</u>   Year 3 <u>5GS & 1PD</u>   Year 4 <u>6GS & 1PD</u>
          Year 5 <u>6GS & 2PD</u>
Cost: Year 1 <u>$140K</u>   Year 2 <u>$175K</u>   Year 3 <u>$250K</u>   Year 4 <u>$300K</u>   Year 5 <u>$405K</u>

Laboratory Assistant(s)
Number: Year 1 _____   Year 2 _____   Year 3 _____   Year 4 _____   Year 5 _____
Cost: Year 1 _____   Year 2 _____   Year 3 _____   Year 4 _____   Year 5 _____

Graduate Assistant(s)
Number: Year 1 _____   Year 2 _____   Year 3 _____   Year 4 _____   Year 5 _____
Cost: Year 1 _____   Year 2 _____   Year 3 _____   Year 4 _____   Year 5 _____

Work Study Student(s)
Number: Year 1 _____   Year 2 _____   Year 3 _____   Year 4 _____   Year 5 _____
Cost: Year 1 _____   Year 2 _____   Year 3 _____   Year 4 _____   Year 5 _____

Other (list): Undergraduate Student (US)
Number: Year 1 <u>1</u>   Year 2 <u>2</u>   Year 3 <u>2</u>   Year 4 <u>3</u>   Year 5 <u>4</u>
Cost: Year 1 <u>$5K</u>   Year 2 <u>$10K</u>   Year 3 <u>$10K</u>   Year 4 <u>$15K</u>   Year 5 <u>$20K</u>

4. What facilities will be required to house these individuals each year? In-house, off-campus, etc. What do you estimate the required square footage to be each year?

Facility	Square Footage
Year 1: <u>Existing Facility</u>	_____
Year 2: <u>Existing Facility</u>	_____
Year 3: <u>Existing Facility</u>	_____
Year 4: <u>Need new office space</u>	<u>100 sq ft</u>
Year 5: <u>Need new office space</u>	<u>100 sq ft</u>

5. What new equipment (computers, software, machines, vehicles, etc.) will you and your staff need each to accomplish the projected tasks and what will the estimated cost be?

New Equipment	Estimated Cost
Year 1: _____	_____
Year 2: _____	_____
Year 3: _____	_____
Year 4: <u>Raman Spectroscopy</u>	<u>$100K</u>
Year 5: <u>FTIR microscopy</u>	<u>$100K</u>

Exhibit 9.2   (*continued*)

6. How many publications will you submit each year and in what journals?

	#	Journal
Year 1:	2	JECS, ES&T
Year 2:	2	ES&T. E&F, EA
Year 3:	5	ES&T, E&F, EA
Year 4:	7	ES&T, E&F, EA
Year 5:	10	ES&T, E&F, EA, PNAS

Books or chapters for publication? If yes, how many and under what titles?

	#	Title
Year 1:	_____	_____
Year 2:	_____	_____
Year 3:	_____	_____
Year 4:	_____	_____
Year 5:	_____	_____

Presentations at conferences/meetings? If yes, how many and at what conferences/meetings?

	#	Conference/Meeting
Year 1:	1	ECS
Year 2:	1	ECS/ANS
Year 3:	3	ECS/ANS/ACS
Year 4:	3	ECS/ANS/ACS
Year 5:	3	ECS/ANS/ACS

7. Based on salary/wages, personnel, and equipment, what is the total amount of resources needed each year? Of this total how much will be requested each year from your organization/institution? How much will be need in grants each year?

	Total	From Organization/Institution	From Grants
Year 1:	$200K	$35K	$165K
Year 2:	$240K	$45K	$195K
Year 3:	$340K	$50K	$290K
Year 4:	$395K	$35K	$360K
Year 5:	$535K	$35K	$500K

Exhibit 9.2 (*continued*)

It is very gratifying when my coachees are positive about getting their personal grants plan outlined (exhibit 9.1) and figuring out how to arrange their time to stay on track. While they continually thank me for assisting them, I know they really do all the work and that I just coach them. I always remind them that having a plan and dedicating the necessary time to stick to it are two of the main ingredients for grants success.

Chapter Ten

Getting Coachees to Focus on the Problem and Measure the Gap

Potential coachees often have to complete an application to be selected for my grants coaching programs. These applications often ask potential program participants to describe the research or project they would like to get funded. After reviewing many of these applications, there is one major weakness that most, if not all, have had in common. They focus too much on their methods and plans for their research and project and not on why it needs to be accomplished.

The coachee knows so much about what they want to do and they neglect to provide information on the gap between what exists now and what could be. This would not be so bad if they only did this on their program applications. But unfortunately, without the appropriate guidance, many grant seekers carry this weakness into their actual proposals. Therefore, an important activity in your first seminar session is to focus on the problem the coachees are looking for a grant to change, reduce, or eliminate.

You must ask them to focus on documenting the problem/gap in detail. This requires them to review the current literature and identify those researchers and institutions doing this work. I ask them to look at more than just the research findings. I ask them to also identify who funded the research and for what amount of money. Most importantly, the coachees need to determine what will happen in the field if the gap is not closed and the problem solved.

Pushing the coachee to define the gap assists him/her in several ways.

1. Focusing on what happens in the field if the gap is not addressed helps to clarify why and who should be interested in closing it. This leads to more key search terms, which can then lead to uncovering more grantors who would like to see the gap reduced.
2. Once the gap is clearly identified, the coaches can begin to determine how closing the gap can be verified, proven, and measured. In 30 percent to 40 percent of my coachees' research/projects, one major problem is finding existing measurement indicators for documenting the change in the problem/gap that are validated or proven. The coachees are so anxious to do their research/projects that they initially think they can simply assume that change will occur and that it will be beneficial.

But you will need to make them aware of the fact that potential grantors would not buy this. Grantors and their reviewers must see that the protocol and methods are really effective. Once coachees acknowledge this, they may decide to focus their first grant on establishing measurement indicators and evaluation tools and verifying them.

Of course, the development of the tools to measure success in closing the gap could be included in a large-scale proposal. However, since many coachees are not currently bringing in large multifaceted grants, starting with an effort to focus on what and how to better document the problem is a good idea. This provides for less-expensive, focused proposals that provide for positioning in the field and/or publications.

In many cases, this exercise forces the coachee to contact those responsible for developing the scales and instruments currently used. They discuss the shortcomings of those measures and their plans to improve upon them. As a result, several of the coachees have been included as Co-PIs on proposals to improve the validation instruments.

Once the problem or subset of the problem that will be the focus of the coachee's efforts has been clearly identified and the plan to document the closure of the gap is valid, the coachee can move on to strategies to develop advocates to endorse the project.

Chapter Eleven

Assisting Coachees in Developing Advocacy Plans, Consortia, and Teams

Most of my coachees suffer from grant-seeking myopia. They want to do their projects/research their way and do not want to involve anyone else in their grants quest. They are taken back when I ask them to explain how they arrived at their particular strategy for dealing with the problem. They do not like it when I ask them if they have investigated and considered any other ways they could conduct their research/project. Chapter 6 in *The "How To" Grants Manual* explores the pros and cons of different approaches to solving problems and estimating the cost for each solution. The contents of this chapter will help coachees explore the costs, advantages, and disadvantages of each potential strategy.

When making preproposal contact with the prospective grantor, I have found it very useful to show three options and their analysis to the grantor. This strategy demonstrates that the coachee is broad-minded and can entertain more than one way to perform the project/research. I encourage coachees to develop approaches that are cost efficient. Completing exhibits 11.1 and 11.2 will be helpful in this effort. Because award sizes and preferred award mechanisms vary from grantor to grantor, these exhibits can be useful in initiating preliminary discussions on the cost benefits for projects/programs and research protocols/approaches.

It is important to get your coachees to think outside of the box and to develop wider angle lenses when approaching potential grantors. This exploration opens the discussion on who and what organizations might be good candidates to approach for assistance in:

- endorsing the grants approach as a timely and/or unique solution to the problem; and
- providing suggestions for improving the proposed solution(s).

My experiences with coachees contacting potential advocates to endorse their proposals and act in an advisory capacity has led to some of the most interesting and productive outcomes. For example, on some occasions these individuals have actually

Summary of Idea and Methodology	Total Cost for Each Idea and Methodology	Total Number of Persons Served for Each Idea and Methodology	Total Cost for Person Served for Each Idea and Methodology	Positive Points of Each Idea and Methodology	Negative Points of Each Idea and Methodology

Exhibit 11.1 Cost–Benefit Analysis Worksheet for Projects/Programs.

become co-principal investigators and co-project directors. I am not suggesting that the coachee should give away his or her grant idea. I am just recommending that he or she discuss the problem and general solution with the potential advisor and ask if this person is interested in endorsing the project.

If the coachee wants to form an advisory group to support his or her proposal, this individual could also be asked to serve in that capacity and even be reimbursed for his or her time and/or travel. However, if the advisory individual is a close colleague, he or she may be willing to provide assistance at no cost. Since an advisory group does not necessarily need to have formal group meetings, the advisory person may not even realize that he or she is part of the coachee's support group and will think that he or she is simply helping out a colleague.

You will need to push your coachees out of their familiar surroundings and encourage them to seek advisers and potential collaborators. Be aware that your coachees will probably provide all types of excuses as to why this strategy will not work and that you will need to assure them that it will.

Summary of Research Protocol/ Approach	Total Cost for Each Research Protocol/Approach	Broad Impacts in Field for Each Research Protocol/Approach	Variables that Present a Challenge for Each Research Protocol/Approach

Exhibit 11.2 Cost–Benefit Analysis Worksheet for Research Protocols/Approaches.

FORMING A TEAM/CONSORTIUM

This is an appropriate time for you, as the coach, to initiate discussions with your coachee as to whether his or her project/research would be more fundable if it were to be carried out by a consortium. The coach should explore with the coachee whether a consortium could provide essential parts of the project with cost savings and enhanced expertise.

My survey of coachees on their experience and formal instruction on how to create excellent functioning teams has shown that 80–90 percent have had little or no training in this area. If fact, most have not had any training or feedback on how their behaviors influence the effectiveness of a team. This underscores the importance of including the half-day team-building seminar outlined in chapter 5 in your sponsor's grants coaching program. In addition, I suggest you review chapter 9 in *The "How To" Grants Manual* and incorporate the team-building exercises described in that chapter in your instruction.

I recommend that you use a commercially produced tool known as the *Team Dimensions Profile* with each of your coachees. The profile is published by John Wiley & Sons and can be ordered from Operations Service Systems, LLC, 702-233-6906, www.SueBeyer.com. Once you have a profile in hand, the following instructions will be clear. I suggest you complete your own profile first to become familiar with the tool.

Start by letting your coachees know there are no correct profiles or answers and that they should answer the questions honestly so that they can become aware of how they are when working with a team to accomplish specific tasks. Before your coachees begin ranking the four statements in each of the twelve groups, have them locate the "rank here" column on their profiles. This is where they rank the "most like themselves" to the "least like themselves," with 4 being the most and 1 being the least. Some coachees invariably put their rankings in the little square boxes instead of on the lines. This is a big mistake.

Do not be surprised when some of your coachees say that none of the choices describe them. Tell them to answer the questions as best as possible and remind them that all four statements in each of the twelve groups must be ranked from 1 to 4. Because this exercise is a failure if the coachees are allowed to go at their own rate, insist that each coachee stop at the bottom of page 3 and wait for the rest of the group to catch up. When all of the coachees have finished ranking the statements on pages 2 and 3, read aloud and follow the instructions on page 4.

It is likely that there will be at least one coachee whose rankings do not total one hundred and twenty. In this case, do not allow anyone to move on. Ask another coachee to take a symbol and add up the numbers again to confirm a total of one hundred and twenty before continuing on. Coachees will need to be reminded that their number in the tally box will not always be found on the axis and that they will need to approximate where the point will fall.

You should take time to discuss page 7 of the profile on approaches and the information on page 8 that outlines the components necessary to construct a balanced grants team utilizing all of the appropriate roles/profiles. For example, while successful proposals offer creative and innovative approaches, having several "creators" on one team can be problematic. They tend to get bored easily, want to move on to a new problem, and are not inclined to enjoy delving into the details that the "executor" is good at. Balancing roles is the key to an effective team.

After administering over one thousand team dimension profiles, I have noticed that the "advancer" role is often underrepresented. This may account for the fact that many coachees are not comfortable to make preproposal contact. I have also noticed that there are usually a considerable number of "refiners" who play the devil's advocate role and critique. "Refiners" need to be reminded that when critiquing a proposal, they need to be sure to include suggestions on how to improve and modify those areas they find fault with.

Ask the coachees to relate what they learned from the profile exercise to their experiences working with team members on grant proposal development and implementation. This discussion could include questions such as:

- What was your best team experience and why?
- What was your worst team experience and why?
- Did the profile exercise shed any light on why these experiences were positive/negative? If so, how?

Each coachee will be very interested in his or her unique profile pattern and will want to determine the one closest to themselves. Therefore, ask each coachee to place a plus (+) by the statements he or she agrees with on his or her pattern and a minus (–) by those he or she disagrees with. You may need to help the coachees identify the pattern that best represents them by having them compare two patterns to determine the one that is most accurate.

Before completing the action plan on page 15 of the *Team Dimensions Profile*, have your coachees review exhibit 11.3, Skills Required to Win Grants. This will help the coachees become aware of the proactive steps necessary to win grants and begin thinking about which profile pattern can best accomplish them. If you like, this can be done as a group exercise by asking your coachees to select the profile that is most appropriate to carry out the tasks involved in proactive winning grants strategies.

Once your coachees are trained in this area and are aware of how individual team preferences and skill sets influence performance, they will not hesitate to use consortia and/or teams to enhance their proposal preparation and implementation.

Developing a winning grants team requires that the members have skills unique to creating a proposal and carrying out the project successfully. Select members by interest and skills. Develop agreed upon rules (attendance, meeting times, recordings, feedback, etc.). Use your Team Dimensions Profile to identify the most appropriate profile patterns for accomplishing the following, proactive grants tasks.

- Brainstorm interventions
- Research grantors
- Get lists of grantees
- Make pre-proposal contact
- Obtain reviewer information
- Update literature search
- Refine intervention/evaluation design
- Develop a project plan/spreadsheet
- Organize a quality circle
- Develop a budget
- Submit reports/milestones/benchmarks to the grantor
- Manage cash flow to avoid over expenditures and/or the need for extensions
- Review job descriptions and conduct performance reviews with grants personnel to comply with grantor policies

Exhibit 11.3   Skills Required to Win Grants.

Chapter Twelve

Encouraging Coachees to Develop and Maintain Research/Grants Profiles

Most universities and many larger nonprofit organizations pay for databases to help those interested in getting grants. These databases are tools to assist grant seekers in locating the most appropriate grantors for their projects/research. When asked by a show of hands how many of the participants in my grants seminars and grants coaching programs have taken advantage of these databases, I have been amazed by the low percentage.

When I have asked why they have not accessed these resources, most have responded that they were unaware of their availability or that they had no time to sign up for and access them. Several universities that use PIVOT (Community of Science) actually enter profiles for all of the faculty- and grants-related staff into the system using a few obvious key search terms. It is expected that grant seekers will go on the site and complete a more specific key word search profile so that they receive the grants alerts that match their profiles.

In my grants coaching programs, I invite the university official in charge of databases to attend the first seminar in my series on finding and winning government grants. I ask him or her to make a brief presentation at the seminar on how the participants/coachees can access the databases available to them. Some are surprised to find out that their profiles have already been entered into a database such as PIVOT with a few obvious key words related to their fields of interest. But most do not have entered profiles, and the majority do not know that such databases even exist.

Review chapter 7 of *The "How To" Grants Manual* on developing key search terms and have your coachees complete exhibit 12.1, the Redefinition/Key Search Terms Worksheet. The successful completion of exhibit 12.1 by your coachees will require some effort on your part because coachees frequently have one grant source in mind and neglect to research other potential grantors. In many cases the grantors they have in mind and the funding vehicles they aim for do not match their (the coachees') credentials, publications, and experience levels. By redefining their proposals, the coachees are forced to locate more likely grantors and/or different funding vehicles.

Many grantors, both public and private, have different vehicles or ways to make a grant under the same program or call for proposals. If your coachee is relatively new

1. *Values*: What words would a grantor use to describe the value of their program to the field?

2. *Subject Area Terms*: Subject areas such as employment, environment, mental health, and child development are used as key search terms in many of the electronic grantor databases. List the subject areas that your project can be related to and/or impacts.

3. *Other Potentially Relevant Fields*: How could you change the focus of your project so that it could be potentially related to more subject areas/fields, and what would these areas/fields be?

4. *Constituency Groups*: Many government and private funding sources focus their grant priorities by the constituency groups they want to impact, such as children, at risk youth, elderly, economically disadvantaged, etc. What constituency group(s) would a funding source have to care about to support your project?

5. *Project Location*: What is the geographic location for your project, and how could you redefine it to better appeal to a grantor's geographic perspective?

   | City/Community | County/Borough/Parish | State |
   | Regional | National | International |

6. *Type of Grant*: What type of grant support are you looking for, and how could you redefine your project to attract grantors interested in different types of support?

Model/Demonstration Project	Research Project	Needs Assessment Grant
Planning Grant	Training Grant	Discretionary
Unsolicited Proposal	Contract	Other

7. *Consortia Partners*: What potential partners/collaborators could you involve to assist in Redefining your project and enhancing your funding perspective? What are the advantages of including them?

Exhibit 12.1   Redefinition/Key Search Terms Worksheet.

in his or her career, he or she could redefine a full research proposal into a multiyear career award or a new investigator grant. Many grants use these different award mechanisms or vehicles to encourage projects that could be ground breaking in the field (i.e., innovative grant awards, innovation research awards, and so on). These award vehicles may be perfect for a new researcher with a grant idea but with limited publications.

Push your coachees to explore how a small change in their grants approach could uncover new and different grantors. Question 1 in exhibit 12.1 encourages the coachee to look at the value of his or her project or research. This is important since funding sources make grants to areas that they value and want to see change.

Question 2 focuses on the more common subject area terms.

Questions 3 and 4 address the issue of redefinition. Could the coachee change the proposal's focus or constituency so that it could appeal to more or better-suited grantors? For example, a coachee interested in teen suicide might find that expanding his or her search terms to include military suicides could result in more potential funding sources.

Question 5 focuses on location. Most coachees focus on finding funding sources in their locale or in the area where they performed the research leading to their terminal degree. However, you need to encourage them to expand the scope of the problem.

This forces them to consider a state-wide, regional, national, or even international focus for their work. Coachees generally want to work with the familiar, smaller, local aspect of their research. To extend further would require lining up other sites, Co-PIs, and/or agencies/institutions. But developing this wider view of the problem and involving others in different areas may be just the right thing to do to increase fundability.

Question 6 deals with the different types of grant support. Encourage your coachees to broaden the scope of their projects. While your coachee may only be considering a research grant, his or her project may be able to be altered slightly to make it a demonstration or training grant. He or she will still be required to measure the impact, and it could still be written up for a journal article as a research outcome.

Question 7 suggests that the coachee consider partners or collaborators to increase fundability. Recently, one of my Alabama-based coachees located a potential grantor that mostly funded projects in Los Angeles. Since her project seemed to fit the grantor's values perfectly, she applied anyway and was asked by the funder if she could locate a Los Angeles collaborator who could apply for the grant for both of them. She said yes, and did, and was ultimately funded.

You should remind your coachees that vocabulary and the common usage of terms vary by the marketplace. Foundations and corporations use different terminology than public (government) funding sources, which must be taken into consideration when coachees develop key words for their search. For example, exhibit 12.2, the Corporate Redefinition Worksheet, is designed to help coachees redefine their projects to specifically attract the interest of and funding from the corporate world. By completing this worksheet, your coachees will come up with several key search terms that can be put together in various combinations and suitable for entry into private grantor databases. Even if your coachees input their key words into their institution's database, the same key words can and will elicit different hits in other databases. Encourage them to submit their key words to a colleague who has access to a different database to see if they get different potential grantors.

You may find that your coachees are reluctant to use one database, let alone several. Therefore, you will need to push them out of their comfort zones and encourage them to talk to colleagues at other institutions to determine what additional databases they may be able to access. While a request to put a few key words in their colleagues' databases will only take a few minutes, the ramifications can be significant. For example, such a request could lead to an advisory/endorsement relationship.

I begin my database discussion with an explanation of the major federal grants database, Grants.gov, and how to use it. (See chapter 13 of *The "How To" Grants Manual*.) I conduct a search in my seminar, and then I take my coachees to their institution's computer lab to conduct their own searches on Grants.gov as well as other government databases, such as the Catalog of Federal Domestic Assistance and Federal Business Opportunities (FedBizOpps). If your coachees do not have access to a commercial database, encourage them to perform an advanced search on Grants.gov. Allowing them to explain how they did this can be a great addition to the section of your seminar that focuses on researching federal grant opportunities.

> 1. How does your intended project/research relate to the concerns of corporate (for profit) grantors? What are your shared values?
> 2. Does or can your project/research provide benefits to corporations in the areas of:
>   - employee development/skill enhancement? If so, how?
>   - employee benefits (including health, quality of life, low costs or risks)? If so, how?
>   - public relations (promotion of a concerned and responsible image in the community)? If so, how?
> 3. Can you redefine your project so that it increases corporate profits by?
>   - promoting a lead to new product development (possible patents, etc.)? If so, explain.
>   - enhancing current products through new applications, redesign, etc.? If so, explain.
>   - increasing sales through product positioning with clients, students, etc.? If so, explain.

Exhibit 12.2   Corporate Redefinition Worksheet.

Even when the private marketplace (foundations and corporations) is seemingly the logical choice for funding your coachees' projects, have them research the $500 billion federal grants marketplace first, since the amount foundations and corporations disperse is significantly less. Private grantors know that the federal government has 90 percent more grant funds to award than they do, and it does not look good if the coachee does not investigate federal opportunities first.

In addition, even if your coachees think their project ideas cannot attract federal funding, they need to be able to tell private grantors they went to the more lucrative federal marketplace first. Sometimes when coachees go to who they believe are the most appropriate federal sources they uncover in their Grants.gov search, they are told that their proposal ideas are great but that they do not match the program's priorities. Coachees can then use this statement when approaching private grantors for support. Coachees can even provide private grantors with their federal reviewers' comments when rejected as proof that they are committed to preparing a more detailed and exacting proposal for their project. Approaching the federal marketplace first shows commitment since preparing a two-page foundation/corporate proposal is easy by comparison.

Review the fee-based databases mentioned in chapter 13 of *The "How To" Grants Manual* with your coachees and determine which one(s) their institution has access to and which one(s) it has purchased. GrantSelect, Sponsored Program Information Network, Pivot (Community of Science), and GrantForward (formerly Illinois Researcher Information Service) are popular. Even if their institution does not subscribe to any of the fee-based grantor databases, they need to be aware of them because they may have colleagues at other institutions who have access to them. Most commercial databases allow, and actually encourage, the sharing of their databases with potential collaborators. Due to the new focus on community engagement with universities many databases even allow for search results to be e-mailed to off-campus addresses.

No matter which databases your coachees have access to, it is crucial for you to encourage them to use them and to enter their key words and research interests into their systems when applicable. Using these databases will provide your coachees with the ability to search for federal opportunities, and in some cases, private grantors. Once their profiles (key words and/or research interests) are entered into the systems some will provide grant alerts of funding sources/programs who may be interested in their proposal area. Some databases even allow for the sharing of research interests among subscribers so that potential collaborators can contact them to discuss possible consortia opportunities.

In addition to these fee-based grants databases, some federal agencies have their own internet mailing lists to electronically disseminate news about their activities and series. (See chapter 13 of *The "How To" Grants Manual*.) If your coachees subscribe to these agencies' e-mail alert services, they can automatically get updated information related to their topics of interest. As a coach, you should encourage the use of these automatic alert systems to keep your coachees in the know and to receive advanced knowledge of upcoming funding opportunities.

Chapter Thirteen

Showing Coachees How to Analyze Federal Grantors to Find the Best Match for Their Research/Projects

This part of the grants coaching process rests firmly on the concept of what proactive grant seeking is all about. Review chapter 14 in *The "How To" Grants Manual* for an explanation of the concept and the techniques required. Provide your coachees with these strategies as part of your government grants seminar. By doing this early on, you can be sure that your coachees will be aware from the onset of your program that the proactive grant-seeking strategies you suggest cannot be successfully employed two or three weeks before a deadline.

Once your coachees have identified several potential federal funding sources, present them with the appropriate steps to analyze these grantors and to select the best choice to fund their research/projects. Ask the coachees to place these proactive strategies on their one-year grants plans. Since the one-year plan integrates the major activities in their professional lives, preproposal contact and analysis of data related to a specific grantor must fit into their already busy schedules.

Download exhibit 13.1, the Federal Grants Research Form, at the beginning of your government grants seminar. Inform your coachees that they will need to complete this form for each federal agency program they plan to approach.

Section 1 of exhibit 13.1 is self-explanatory. You will need to remind your coachees how important it is for them to obtain the program description from the CFDA, and the synopsis and full announcement from Grants.gov. In addition, coachees often forget to subscribe to automatic e-mail alerts and notifications. Stress that this step is crucial to keeping up-to-date on program information.

Checklist 1 in section 2 of the exhibit requires the coachee to obtain information that will help him or her analyze past grantees. This includes obtaining a list of those who have recently received funding and then contacting at least one of these individuals. Let your coachees know that lists of past grantees are available on Grants.gov and on funding agency websites.

After carefully reviewing full program descriptions and announcements and analyzing past grantees, your coachee may eliminate some of his or her prospective grantors because he or she has already determined that there is a weak match between his or

Section 1
For (Your Project Reference or Title): _____
CFDA No. _____
Grants.gov Funding No. _____
Government Agency: _____
Deadline Date(s): _____

Create a file for each program you are researching and place all information you gather on this program in the file. Use this Federal Grants Research Form to:

- keep a record of the information you have gathered
- maintain a log of all contact made with the federal program

Agency Address: _____
Agency Director: _____ Program Director: _____
Name/Title of Contact Person: _____
Telephone Number: _____ Fax Number: _____
Email: _____ Web Site: _____

In order to prepare a professional proposal, you need to gather the information listed below. Place a check mark next to the information you have gathered and placed in the file.

__ Program description from *CFDA*
__ Synopsis from Grants.gov
__ Subscription for automatic email alert/notification for up-to-date program info.
__ Copy of full announcement (link on Grants.gov)

Section 2 – Checklist of Steps to Grants Success

1. Analyze past grantees (attach completed exhibit 13.2 to this form)
   __ Obtain list of past grantees
   __ Contact past grantee
2. Analyze evaluation/scoring rubric
   __ Obtain evaluation/scoring rubric to be used on your proposal (attach copy to this form)
3. Analyze proposal review process
   __ Gather information of the reviewers and the proposal review process
   __ Contact past reviewer
4. Analyze successful proposals
   __ Procure samples of successful pre-proposals and full proposals
5. Confirm prospect research through contact with grantor
   __ Contact public funding source official via phone or e-mail
   __ Make appointment with a public funding source official
   __ Visit a public funding source official
6. Make your decision to develop a proposal and to apply to a specific federal grant program
   ___ Evaluate each potential grantor and tailor your approach and funding request

Exhibit 13.1   Federal Grants Research Form.

her project and who and what the grantor funds. However, if the match appears sound at this point, your coachee should continue to gather information on the program.

Checklist 2 has to do with analyzing scoring rubrics. Information on scoring rubrics can be found in program descriptions and full announcements. This is why it is crucial for your coachees to procure these items for each program they are interested in. It is imperative that your coachees know what the scoring rubric or criterion is before they construct their proposals. They need to know that it is not what they write, but rather how they write, that will be evaluated/scored.

Checklist 3 calls for a continued focus on the review process. You should suggest that the coachees learn as much as possible about the background of the reviewers and encourage them to contact colleagues who have been reviewers. This will allow them to learn more about what the funding source is looking for and how best to write their proposals toward the readers/reviewers.

Checklist 4 asks coachees to analyze samples of successful preproposals and full proposals. These can often be found on agency websites. And, in some instances, past grantees who are contacted by potential grantees will share their successful proposals.

Checklist 5 suggests that the coachee makes preproposal contact with his or her potential grantor to confirm the accuracy of the prospect research he or she has gathered.

Once all of the steps in exhibit 13.1 have been completed and all of the analysis has been done, your coachee will be ready to make his or her decision concerning whether to develop a full proposal tailored to a specific federal grant program.

Exhibit 13.2, the Program and Past Recipient Analysis Worksheet, must be completed by your coachee for each program under consideration. Completion of this worksheet should be done in conjunction with the completion of exhibit 13.1 so that unsuitable grantors can be eliminated before more time is invested in futile prospect research.

Question 1 in exhibit 13.2 asks for the number of applications received and the number of applications awarded. By comparing these two numbers, your coachee will have a rough idea of his or her likelihood of success. Unfortunately, many programs do not provide information on the number of applicants. However, this figure can be estimated if the program provides the percent of proposals funded. For example, if the program had a 10 percent award rate last year and thirty proposals were funded, it would be fair to assume, based on last year's figures, that your coachee's proposal may be in competition with three hundred others. To get a more accurate figure, your coachee could ask about the number of applications versus the number awarded in preproposal contact with the grantor. However, they should be aware that some program officers might feel like they are calculating the odds and they, the program officers, may not like that.

Based on a few personal experiences, I still recommend trying to get an estimate for success. For instance, I once invested a lot of time in pursuing a grant from a relatively new program with no recorded track record of past successes. Ultimately, I discovered too late that in the previous year it had funded two proposals out of one thousand applications, which made my chances of success highly unlikely!

Many government programs are now requiring prospective grantees to submit a preproposal application before being invited to submit a full proposal. Encourage your coachees to obtain a copy of a successful preproposal application so they can get an idea of what the grantor likes in terms of format, and so on.

1. Applications
    - How many applications were received? _____
    - How many applications were funded? _____

2. Award Size
    - What was the largest award granted? _____
      For what type of project? _____
      For how many years? _____
    - What was the smallest award granted? _____
      For what type of project? _____
      For how many years? _____

3. Grantor Type
    - What characteristics or similarities can be drawn from last year's list of grant recipients?
    - What is the size and type of grantee organization (i.e., public, private, college)?
    - What are the geographic preferences or concentrations?

4. Project Director/Principal Investigator
    - What title or degrees appear most frequently on the list of last year's recipients?
    - Does there seem to be a relationship between award size and project director degree?

5. From the list of last year's grantees, select 4 or 5 to contact for more information. Select grantees that you may have a link with and/or organizations that you are familiar with.

6. Based on the information gathered in question 1-4, rate how well your proposal idea matches the prospective grantor's profile.
    _____ very well   _____ good   _____ fair   _____ not well

Exhibit 13.2   Program and Past Recipient Analysis Worksheet.

Question 2 in exhibit 13.2 asks the coachee to analyze the prospective grantor's preferred award sizes. Responses to this question will help the coachee determine how well his or her award request fits the funding source's award profile. If the amount of funding the coachee requires does not match the grantor's pattern, he or she may decide to eliminate it from his or her prospect list.

The purpose of question 3 is to allow the coachee to develop a profile of the successful grantee type and to compare it to his or her project. If the preferred type of grantee does not match with your coachee's institution or geographic location, he or she could look for a collaborator that could serve as the lead organization. In that case, your coachee could then act as a partner, Co-PI, or a consultant.

Question 4 is designed to provide a picture or description of the grantor's preferred qualifications for project directors/principal investigators. Answers to these questions will show your coachee who he is she is competing against and how his or her qualifications stack up in comparison.

> From: <grantseeker@proactive.edu>
> To: <successful past grantee>
> Cc:
> Sent: Date, Time
> Subject: Request for Copy of Funded Proposal
>
> Dear [Successful Grantee]:
>
> I obtained your name from the list of grantees under the _____ program. I am sure you are very pleased over your success and your award. I am working on a proposal for the same program in a related, but different, area. (You could add more about your area here.)
>
> Since you are funded and we are not in competition, I am hoping you will share of copy of your winning proposal with me. (If there was a pre-proposal application also ask for it.) I would like to review it for style, format, and the best way to address the criteria components. Naturally, I expect you to withhold any specific information you feel is proprietary.
>
> It would also be very helpful if you could include your reviewers' comments to help me focus on what they are looking for.
>
> I look forward to receiving your materials and also to learning about your results and possible presentation at a shared convention.
>
> Name
> Title
> Organization/Institution
> Address
> Phone Number
> Fax Number

Exhibit 13.3   Sample E-mail to a Past Grantee Requesting a Copy of His/Her Successful Proposal.

Question 5 has to do with preproposal contact with past grantees. Require your coachees to contact several past grantees to obtain more information about their successful proposals. Before they do so, have them scrutinize their list of past grantees, looking for anyone on the list whom they may know, have met at professional meetings, and/or are from institutions they have relationships with. Obviously, these would be the best candidates for them to contact.

Once they have identified four or five, have them send e-mails to request a copy of their successful proposals. Exhibit 13.3 is a sample e-mail they can tailor to their own specifications. Chapter 14 of *The "How To" Grants Manual* provides detailed information on approaching successful grant recipients, what to request from them, and a list of suggested questions to ask to learn more about the funding source.

Question 6 asks the coachee to assess how well his or her proposal idea matches the prospective grantor's profile. Remind your coachee that the accuracy of this

```
CFDA # _____          Prospect Rating      A. Excellent
    Program Title _____                    B. Good
    Amount Requested _____                 C. Fair
    Percent Match/In-Kind _____
                                        Estimated Success   A. 75%
                                                            B. 50%
                                                            C. 25%
```

1. How does your grant request match with the average award size to your
   type of organization? _____
   size of organization? _____
   location of organization? _____
   proposal focus? _____

2. What was the number of applications received versus the number of grants awarded
   in your area of interest?
   applications received? _____
   grants awarded? _____

3. How does your organization compare to the previous grantees relative to
   expertise of key individuals? _____
   publications and previously funded proposals? _____
   access to special equipment, space, etc.? _____
   access to subjects? _____

4. How would you rate the funding staff's interest in your concept?
   __ very interested __ interested __ not interested __ unknown

5. From the information you obtained on the reviewers and the review process, what should
   your writing strategy include?

6. Based on the information you obtained on the review process, how will points be
   distributed in the funding source's evaluation process?

   Area   Point Value
   _____   _____
   _____   _____
   _____   _____

Exhibit 13.4 Tailoring Worksheet.

assessment will be based on the thoroughness of his or her analysis of the prospective funding source.

Have your coachees complete the tailoring worksheet (exhibit 13.4) to:

- further analyze each grant or program they are interested in;
- rate each prospect; and
- select the closest matches.

Remind your coachees that there will seldom be a perfect fit between their projects and their potential grantors' programs. However, it is likely that with some tailoring and tweaking of their projects, their chances of success will increase.

Having your coachees analyze specific characteristics of their prospective federal grantors and past successful recipients adds a new level of sophistication to their grants behavior. It moves them from focusing on what they want to do to focusing on who their prospective grantors have funded in the past, the characteristics of the grants they have awarded, what they are likely to fund in the future, and how well their (the coachees) projects match the grantors' desires.

Chapter Fourteen

Assisting Coachees in Contacting Federal Program Officers

Getting your coachees to leave the comfort of their professional homes and contact past grantees is difficult. In my experience many coachees have problems making this contact and require persistent reinforcement in this area. But getting coachees to make preproposal contact with federal program officers is even harder. In chapter 4, I suggest making preproposal contact with federal program officers a grants coaching program requirement. This area is so important that it deserves its own chapter.

From the coachees' perspectives, all they really want to do is write-up their proposal/research ideas and get funded to do them. They may see the need to search for the most likely grantors. However, they will probably view the other proactive grant-seeking steps as superfluous. That is until you work through the steps with them and provide insight on how the accomplishment of the steps will help them get funded. They will buy into the process after they see the benefits. Up to now, the benefits have been very tangible. Of course it makes sense to contact past grantees to gain insight into the grantor and to procure a copy of a funded proposal. But now you are asking your coachee to contact the person with the money, make an appointment, and visit them in a strange and huge bureaucracy—Washington, D.C.

Your job gets difficult at this point. It is not the mandate of making preproposal contact that helps the coachee have a successful experience. It is how you get the coachee ready and as comfortable as possible with this task. In one instance I even traveled to D.C. with my coachee to meet with program officers. Before our visit I used the materials in *The "How To" Grants Manual* to develop relevant questions. I even performed a role play whereby I acted as the program officer.

In the first visit I led the conversation and asked the pertinent questions we derived from the research on past grants, contact with grantees, and discussions with a previous reviewer who was on our faculty.

The next appointment was led by the coachee. She was introverted, and while a little uncomfortable, asked relevant questions that demonstrated she had done her research. The program officer was impressed with her knowledge of the program and was intrigued with her proposal idea. We had requested 15 minutes of the program officer's time, but he gave us forty-five minutes. After leaving, my coachee remarked that she thought she did a great job at asking inductive, thoughtful questions. I assured her that the reasons for her success were the passion for her research, her preappointment homework, the quality of her questions, and her straightforward approach.

As the experienced coach knows, program officers have busy schedules and do not like to waste time going over something that is on their program's website or in the application guidelines. However, they will respond positively to honest questions and well-prepared applicants.

Review the materials on pages 159–69 of *The "How To" Grants Manual* and encourage your coachees to perform the following steps.

1. Contact public funding sources via the telephone or e-mail months before the deadline and more than once if necessary.

   Progam officers have told me that only about 20 percent of prospective grantees send a follow-up e-mail or make a follow-up phone call if they do not respond. Make sure your coachees keep trying to get through. Instill the importance of persistence in your coachees and make them aware of the fact that studies have demonstrated that contact with program officers prior to submission increases success rates by threefold.
2. Make an appointment to see the public funding source official.

   Let your coachees know that the optimum benefit is gained from face-to-face contact.
3. Visit the public funding source.

   The coach needs to leave nothing to chance here. Role-play the questions to be asked. Be sure your coachee starts questions with a statement that reflects his or her research that led up to the inquiry. Exhibit 14.1 provides questions that both myself and my coachees have used. Review these, and then help your coachee to develop his or her own questions. Remind him or her that program officers like to be of help by answering questions. They do not want to give out privileged information that could provide an advantage, but they do not mind answering questions that clarify various aspects of their program.

Review the materials the coachee plans to use. Determine back-up plans if audiovisuals are going to play a critical part in his or her presentation.

Discuss with your coachees the dress required for a Washington, D.C. visit to a federal program officer. D.C. is very conservative when it comes to clothing. In general, it is no place for jeans and sneakers. This is a delicate area to discuss and may even press your coaching skills, but it must be addressed. I tell my coachees that the importance of their project/research warrants making sure that the messenger's appearance does not discredit the message.

Coachees should know that they can use the fact that they are enrolled in a grants coaching program to their advantage. They can mention to the program officer that answers to their questions will be shared with their fellow coachees. In addition, they can use the requirements of the grants coaching program as a basis for their inquiries. For example, they can say they are requesting information on the scoring rubric because it is a program requisite and that they are required to share the information with their fellow

- I have located the program application on your website and found references to [*rules, announcements, and so on*]. Are there any other sources of information I should review?
- The [*CFDA, Grants.gov, or agency publication*] lists the program funding level at [*$$$$*]. Do you expect that to change?
- My research shows that there are several different types of awards that fall under your program and this area of interest. What are the differences in the success rates (applications versus awards) in the granting mechanisms your program uses? [In addition to research and demonstration grants, many programs have special awards for young or new researchers or career awards to initiate and shape a career. The rules for qualifying for each type of granting mechanism vary, as does the funding. All of the variables must be taken into consideration when deciding to apply to a program or a specific type of grant award.]
- How will successful grantees from last year affect the chances for new or first applicants? Will last year's grantees compete with new grantees, or have their funds been set aside? If their funds have been set aside, how much is left for new awards?
- Are there any unannounced programs or unsolicited proposal funds in your agency to support an important project like ours?
- The required matching portion is [*X*] percent. Would it improve our chances for funding if we provide a greater portion than this?
- The program announcement states that matching funds are suggested but not mandatory. I need to give my institution an idea of how much match is needed to meet the "suggested" amount. Could you provide me with a figure, or select three past grantees at random, and tell me how much match the grantees provided?
- If no match is required, would it help our proposal if we volunteered to cost share?
- What is the most common mistake or flaw in the proposals you receive?
- We have developed several approaches to this needs area. From your vantage point, you may know whether one of our approaches has been funded but not yet published. Could you review our concept paper and give us any guidance?
- Would you review or critique our proposal if we get it to you early?
- Would you recommend a previously funded proposal for us to read for format and style? [Your coachees are entitled to see funded proposals, but they still should be mannerly when asking.]
- What changes do you expect in type or number of awards this year (for example, fewer new awards versus continuing awards)?
- We will conduct a quality circle (mock review) to improve our proposal before we submit it. Could we get more information on the review process your office will conduct? Can we get a reviewers' package including instructions, scoring information, weighing of criteria, and so on? What is the background of the reviewers? How are the reviewers selected? How many proposals do reviewers read? How much time do they take to read and score each proposal?
- How are multiple applications to different programs in your agency that use the same basic proposal viewed?
- How is the project director's or principal investigator's commitment to other proposals viewed by your staff and the peer reviewers? [For example, a fellow of mine was included in a pending proposal for 5 percent of his time. He was told by his institution's research office that his commitment precluded him from applying to this particular federal program as the project director for his own proposal. I instructed him to contact the program officer and he learned he could apply if he agreed to drop the 5 percent commitment if he was awarded his grant that called for 50 percent of his time.]

Exhibit 14.1   Possible Questions to Ask a Federal Program Officer.

coachees. Many program officers have gone through some sort of mentorship and/or fellows' program and understand how important the sharing component is. Hence, they may feel a little more inclined or even obligated to provide the requested information.

Encourage the coachees to complete exhibit 14.2 to be sure they are bringing the correct materials, advocates, and staff to their visit. In addition, they should use exhibit 14.3

Before each visit to a funding source, review this sheet to be sure you are taking the correct materials, advocates and staff.

Agency Director: _____   E-mail: _____
Program Director: _____   E-mail: _____
Contact Person: _____   E-mail: _____

Education: College _____
            Post-graduate _____
Work Experience: _____
Military Experience: _____
Service Clubs: _____
Interests/Hobbies: _____
Publications: _____

Comments:

[Note: Do not ask the staff person direct questions related to these areas. Instead, record information that has been volunteered or gathered from observations made in the office.]

Exhibit 14.2 Funding Source Staff Profile.

Project Title: _____

Complete a public funding source contact summary sheet each time you contact a public funding source.

Agency Name: _____

Program Officer: _____

Contacted On (Date): _____

By Whom: _____

Contacted By: _____ Letter _____ Phone _____ E-mail _____ Personal Visit

Staff or Advocate Present: _____

Discussed:

Results:

Exhibit 14.3 Public Funding Source Contact Summary Sheet.

Prospect Rating:
   A. Excellent
   B. Good
   C. Fair

Estimated Success:
   A. 75%
   B. 50%
   C. 25%

1. How does your grant request match with the average award size to your
   type of organization? _____
   size of organization? _____
   location of organization? _____
   proposal focus? _____

2. What was the number of applications received versus the number of grants awarded in your area of interest?
   applications received _____
   grants awarded _____

3. How does your organization compare to the previous grantees relative to
   expertise of key individuals? _____
   publications and previously funded proposals? _____
   access to special equipment, space, etc.? _____
   access to subjects? _____

4. How would you rate the funding staff's interest in your concept?
   _____ very interested
   _____ interested
   _____ not interested
   _____ unknown

5. From the information you obtained on the reviewers and the review process, what should your writing strategy include?

6. Based on the information you obtained on the review process, how will points be distributed in the funding source's evaluation process? List area and associated points.

Exhibit 14.4 Tailoring Worksheet.

to record their contact with program officers. Exhibit 14.4 is the final step in directing the coachees' efforts to select the best grantor to pursue. By completing the analysis requested on this worksheet, the coachees will be able to rate their prospects and estimate their success. Now, your coachees are ready for planning the successful federal proposal.

Chapter Fifteen

Guiding Coachees through the Federal Proposal Development Process

Coachees make four major mistakes when it finally comes down to creating their federal proposals. First, they prefer to write the proposal their way. They must be coached to carefully review the guidelines, refer to the scoring rubric, and examine several funded proposals for format, style, and so on.

The second mistake they commonly make is using their vocabulary in their proposal instead of crafting it toward what they have learned about the backgrounds of the actual reviewers.

Coachees also often mistakenly move to their protocol, methods, and what they want to do before clearly establishing the need and identifying the gap that exists in the field. While many coachees will cite the latest literature in their field, they often do not arrange the data in a way that makes the reviewer conclude that something must be done. By moving quickly to what the coachee wants to do, the reason to close the gap between what is and what should be is weakened and the proposal fails to motivate the reviewer to fund it. To avoid this issue, the coach should role-play being the reviewer and, as such, ask the coachee to explain the reasons why a reviewer would find his or her proposal compelling. The coachee should be able to identify who will be affected and how if the proposal does not get funded and what will be lacking in the field if the project is not accomplished.

Finally, coachees often have a hard time telling the funding source why they should be the PI, PD, or Co-PI of their project. They often shy away from providing specific accomplishments or reasons why they should be funded. Just wanting to do the research is not a good enough reason. They must answer why they should be funded, and their answer must be convincing. To help them do this, I require each of my coachees to introduce themselves to their fellow coachees as if their fellow coachees were the grantor and then state why they should be funded, what their uniquenesses are, how they are qualified to do the work required in the proposal, and even why their institution should be funded. To further assist your coachees with this critical step, review chapter 8 of *The "How To" Grants Manual* and have your coachees complete exhibit 15.1.

> Federal and state proposal applications require information on your organization's ability to perform the tasks you outline in your proposal. Your unique qualities or attributes are what enable you to perform these tasks. The sections of government applications that require this information are sometimes referred to as *Adequacy of Institutional Resources and Quality of Project Personnel.*
>
> On government applications, these sections may be assigned a point value. While these components may not be mandatory on foundation and corporate proposals, the information they contain is equally important in convincing private funding sources that your organization is the right grantee for them.
>
> What makes your organization uniquely suited to carry out the work outlined in your proposal? How will you provide the grantor with the assurance it will receive a job well done?
>
> 1. *Adequacy of Institutional Resources*: Please list the positive qualities and uniquenesses that your organization or institution possesses that will ensure a grantor that you are the best place to do the job. When applicable, include factors such as:
>
>   - relevance of purpose and mission
>   - geographic location
>   - relationship and availability to subject population
>   - presence of animal laboratories
>   - data analysis capabilities
>   - _____
>   - _____
>   - _____
>
> 2. *Quality of Project Personnel*: Please list the unique qualifications of your project personnel. Take into consideration factors such as:
>
>   - years of related experience
>   - number of publications and presentations
>   - awards and special recognition
>   - number and dollar amounts of funded grants & contracts
>   - _____
>   - _____
>   - _____

Exhibit 15.1 Uniqueness Worksheet.

I do not spend a lot of time in my seminars discussing how to write hypotheses, specific aims, program objectives, methods, or protocols unless I am specifically requested to do so. Instead, I strongly encourage my seminar participants and coachees to procure several previously funded proposals and use them as models to replicate. By reviewing funded applications, they can see how successful grantees constructed the proposal parts and how they worked other winning concepts into their proposals.

Chapter 15 of *The "How To" Grants Manual* provides an explanation of the most common terms used for the various proposal components. When I first began teaching grant seminars I went into great detail on techniques for writing program objectives. For example, the writer must first determine the result areas, measurement indicators, performance standards, time frame, and cost. Then the objective can be written in the standard format as follows: "To [action verb and statement reflecting the measurement indicator] by [performance standard] by [deadline] at a cost of no more than [cost frame]." However, when I started to review funded proposals, I noticed they often included methods instead of objectives.

When I asked a grantor about this apparent lack of proper objective construction, he told me he did not care about what I liked or what I taught. He just wanted prospective grantees to do it his way. Hence, I cannot stress enough the importance of encouraging your coachees to review funded proposals and use them as models. If your coachees really need to spend more time understanding objectives, hypotheses, research questions, and/or specific aims, by all means use the material in *The "How To" Grants Manual* to assist them. However, I still think it is more useful to follow the concepts found in winning proposals rather than complying with "my" way.

The one other technique that I encourage my coachees to incorporate is the development of a spreadsheet to help them:

- outline their project;
- develop their budgets;
- create budget narratives;
- defend their budgets;
- provide job descriptions for project personnel;
- project monthly and quarterly cash forecasts;
- identify matching or in-kind contributions;
- provide a timeline outlining milestones and progress indicators; and
- develop a plan for proposal completion.

Any spreadsheet that provides these functions is fine. However, the spreadsheet I have developed and use is called the project planner. A downloadable Microsoft Excel version of this spreadsheet is available free of charge at www.dgbauer.com. Sample project planners and an explanation of how to complete a project planner can be found in chapter 15 of *The "How To" Grants Manual*.

I encourage you to have your coachees fill out a rough draft of their spreadsheet at the onset of proposal development to help identify and list the methods they plan to employ in completing their project. Ultimately, using a project planner will help avoid many of the problems inherent in initiating and carrying out a project by requiring the coachee to deal with the scope and sequence of the steps he or she must take to formulate a winning federal proposal.

Now, onto your role in improving your coachees' federal proposals.

Chapter Sixteen

The Coach's Role in Improving Federal Proposals

This chapter deals with how the coach can make a dramatic difference in the quality and, hence, the acceptance rate of his or her coachees' proposals. Over the last thirty years my workshops have included having the seminar participants review parts of proposals and make suggestions for improvement. From doing this, it has become obvious to me that grant seekers need to learn how to:

- use the grantor's scoring rubric to evaluate and score each section of a proposal rather than give one overall score. An overall rating of very good would not yield an excellent unless the proposal writer knew which parts were excellent and should remain untouched and which parts were only good and could be improved.
- appeal to the backgrounds of the reviewers and write to the real readers. Most grant seekers write to themselves by using their vocabulary and their level of expertise.
- accept feedback on their proposal as a positive experience. To assist in this effort, I changed the name of my seminar exercise from proposal critiquing to proposal improvement. As a coach you must help your coachees welcome proposal feedback and suggestions for improvement rather than fear them. My goal with my coachees is to actually have them feel disappointed when they do not have the opportunity to receive valuable feedback.

I suggest you review the section on improving federal proposals in *The "How To" Grants Manual* (chapter 16) and the section on improving proposals being submitted to private grantors (chapter 25). The information in these chapters provides the rationale, examples, and exhibits that are the basis for helping your coachees improve their proposals.

You may be interested in knowing where this concept for proposal improvement is derived from. Post–World War II left Japan's industries in ruins. The United States government assisted in rebuilding Japan's commerce by having Japan apply Walter Edward Demings's concept of total quality management (TQM) to improve their goods and make their workers accountable for the products they created.

What's particularly noteworthy is that the TQM concept was embraced by both the Japanese workers and the management. Workers were invited to attend short sessions or meetings after their shifts to explore how they could produce a better product more efficiently. The lesson to learn here is that responsibility for quality became so important to these workers that they voluntarily chose to attend these sessions—even after working a long, hard shift!

So, how can you use the TQM concept with your coachees to improve their product or goods (i.e., their proposals)? I suggest you incorporate the TQM concept into what I call quality circles. To do this, require your coachees to take part in the lecture-based seminar on improving grant proposals through quality circles as outlined in chapter 5 of this book. This seminar presents the expectations and rules for conducting a quality circle. The concepts are practiced in a quality circle/mock review exercise using the coachees' own proposals.

This exercise has been a very rewarding experience for my coachees. The changes made in their proposals that resulted from this exercise have proven to be instrumental in gaining higher scores and increasing fundability. You will better understand and appreciate the power of this strategy after you read the comments in *The "How To" Grants Manual* that administrators have made concerning the use of quality to improve proposals at their institutions (chapter 16, pages 212–13).

Administrators of some of my coaching programs have documented and credited the use of quality circles with their 50 percent plus funding rates. While I cannot say that this success is due totally to this proactive step, I can say that improvements made in conjunction with quality circles have resulted in very positive responses from reviewers with regard to proposal clarity, ease of reading, and attention to detail.

While my experience has shown that the quality circle exercise produces great results when it is conducted with coachees in a grants coaching program, the real benefits accrue when coachees share the concept with colleagues not enrolled in the program. Through the use of quality circles, your grants coaching has the potential to reach beyond your current class of coachees. It is amazing to think of what could be possible at an institution that buys into the idea of quality circles. The use of quality circles has the potential to impact an entire institution even beyond superior grant-seeking results. For example, if your quality circle work with several cohorts of coachees can change the way an institution views its mission, you have really done something useful and you should feel gratified.

The successful use of the quality circle model requires you to be true to the concept by making sure you are teaching your coachees how to improve proposals, not critique them. To really work, a quality circle must be based on positivism, not negativism. Many of my coachees who have experienced a positive lift from their quality circle have introduced the concept to their colleagues. Unfortunately, some were disappointed with the outcome of their actions. I had to remind those disillusioned coachees that the atmosphere in some higher-education institutions and other organizations revolves around critiquing what is wrong, determining what is wrong, and dwelling on the negative.

To counteract this negative construct, the most important rule when conducting a quality circle is to focus on a proposal's positive points first. Quality circle participants should not even be asked to identify the proposal's problem areas. Instead, they should be asked to provide the proposal writer with ways to improve the proposal. That means that if the mock reviewer (quality circle participant) believes that a particular section of the proposal is good, he or she should provide the proposal writer with ways to make it even better so it has a greater chance of receiving a higher score from the real reviewers. While the way the exercise is presented may seem trivial, it is monumental in creating a positive atmosphere that has the potential to lead to a more fundable proposal.

When my coachees want to replicate the quality circle construct with staff who have not been through the training seminar and an individual quality circle, I suggest that at least two trained coachees lead the exercise. This will ensure that the experience stays positive and does not turn into a negative situation where the grant seeker feels he or she must defend his or her proposal.

Your coachees can use exhibit 16.1 or a tailored version of it to invite individuals to participate in a grants quality circle. Exhibit 16.2 can be e-mailed to the quality circle participants as an attachment to help them role-play being a real reviewer and reading the proposal from the real reviewer's point of view and not their own. It should also be pointed out to the mock reviewers that it does not do the proposal writer any good to invest more time reading the proposal than the actual reviewer will.

In addition, it has been my experience that mock reviewers may not want to score each section of the proposal. Toward this end, I ask my coachee (proposal writer) to designate the sections that should be read and scored before moving on to the next

---

Date

Name
Address

Dear _____:

I would like to take this opportunity to request your input in helping our [institution, organization, group, team] submit the very best grant proposal possible. We are asking that you review the enclosed proposal from the federal reviewer's viewpoint. The attached materials will help you role-play the actual manner in which the proposal will be evaluated.

Please read the information on the reviewers' backgrounds and the scoring system, and limit the time you spend reading the proposal to the time constraints that the real reviewers will observe. A grants quality circle worksheet has been provided to assist you in recording your scores and comments.

A meeting of all mock reviewers composing our quality circle has been scheduled for [date]. Please bring your grants circle worksheet with you to this meeting. The meeting will last for less than one hour. Its purpose is to analyze the scores and brainstorm suggestions to improve this proposal.

Sincerely,

Name
Phone Number

Exhibit 16.1   Sample Letter/E-mail Inviting an Individual to Participate in a Grants Quality Circle.

The following information is designed to help you develop the proper focus for the review of the attached proposal.

1. Review Panelists
   Proposals are read by review panelists with the following degrees and backgrounds:
   Degrees: _____
   Backgrounds (Age, Viewpoints, Biases, etc.): _____
   _____

2. The Time Element and Setting
   Number of proposals read by each reviewer: _____
   Average length of time spent reading each proposal: _____
   Proposals are read at the:
   __ reviewer's home __ reviewer's work __ funder's location __ other site

3. The Scoring System
   The scoring system that will be employed is based on a scale of: _____
   The areas to be scored are (list or include attachment):
   Area: _____ Total Possible Points ____ Your Score ____
   Area: _____ Total Possible Points ____ Your Score ____
   Area: _____ Total Possible Points ____ Your Score ____
   Area: _____ Total Possible Points ____ Your Score ____
   Area: _____ Total Possible Points ____ Your Score ____

   According to the total points per area, how many points represent an outstanding, superior, adequate, weak or poor score? For example, if the total points possible for one area are 25, 0-8 = poor, 9-12 = weak, 13-19 = adequate, 20-23 = superior, and 24-25 = outstanding. _____
   _____

   After recording your scores, list the positive points of the proposal that may appeal to the actual reviewer. Also list those areas that seem weak and cost valuable points. List suggestions for improvement. _____
   _____
   _____
   _____

Exhibit 16.2   Federal/State Grants Quality Circle Worksheet.

section. Exhibit 16.3 identifies the role of the quality circle group facilitator, the proposal writer, and the quality circle participants/mock reviewers.

In my programs, the coachees are required to create a draft proposal and to allow it to be evaluated as part of the quality circle classroom experience. Frequently, time does not allow for all of the coachees' proposals to be reviewed in the quality circle exercise. Depending on the time that is set aside for this exercise and how knowledgeable the participants are of the proposal topic, you may need to limit the sections of the proposal that will be reviewed.

For example, some proposals may include an explanation of methods or protocols that is beyond the expertise of the mock reviewers. In this case, evaluation of that

> **Group Facilitator**
>
> The group leader or facilitator is responsible for keeping the group on task, having the group focus on the proposal's positive aspects before moving on to those that need to be improved, and reinforcing a constructive learning atmosphere. The facilitator may engage in reading and scoring the sections as well, but should reserve his or her comments and scores till last. The group leader may decide to facilitate discussion only if the is her or her desire.
>
> The facilitator will request the scores for each section or part of the proposal before asking for the positive areas and areas to be improved. The facilitator is advised to rotate the request for comments to start each section among the participants, and to encourage everyone to participate. The facilitator will set a constructive tone and learning focus by asking each participant for his or her positive comments first, and will interrupt any participant who moves to the areas to be improved before each participant has presented his or her comments. After all positive comments have been presented the focus will turn to the areas that need to be improved to raise the score for each section.
>
> **Proposal Initiators/Writers**
>
> The creators of the proposal under review may choose to either attend the quality circle meeting, or not be present and just receive the results. If present, they should not be allowed to interrupt the process, defend the proposal, or provide any additional information except for a short introduction providing the participants with information they learned through preproposal contact or from successful grantees or past reviewers. This information will help prepare the participants for the review. The creators may also ask questions to clarify points at the conclusion of the discussion on each of the sections to be reviewed.
>
> **Quality Circle Participants**
>
> The exercise participants are expected to adhere to the suggestions on reading time frames, development of helpful comments, and the scoring of each section. They are allowed to raise question, but asking questions of the proposal initiators should be kept to a minimum and allowed only when necessary to promote a realistic review.

Exhibit 16.3   Conducting a Quality Circle Review/Roles.

section can be eliminated. Since the title and the abstract/summary are critical in how the proposal is perceived by the grantor and the reviewers, these sections should always be looked at in the quality circle. Of course, in the real evaluation the reviewers will read, comment on, and score all of the proposal sections.

   I suggest you allow each quality circle participant to play the role of the group facilitator at least once so all of them can experience trying to keep the participants on the positive aspects of the proposal before moving to the areas to improve. As you coach multiple groups, reading multiple proposals, you will hear some participants talk about sections of proposals that they really dislike or think are terrible. Encourage these participants to frame their comments positively instead of negatively. Even when discussing the areas needing improvement, your coachees should suggest ways the proposal could be amended and enhanced so that it ultimately receives an excellent rating.

It is difficult for proposal writers to remain in the room when their proposals are being evaluated. However, I instruct them to stay and to float around the room like a fly on the wall. They are not to answer any questions since in the actual review they will not be present to clear up any confusion or misunderstandings.

The group facilitator should be provided with feedback on each section of the proposal as it is reviewed. As the coach, I walk the room, keep track of how each quality circle is proceeding, and watch and listen for how well the facilitator is keeping the group on a positive perspective. The facilitator should:

- hand out copies of the proposal and instruct the participants to make their comments in the margin of the proposal;
- start each section evaluation with a score based on the grantor's rubric;
- ask each participant to provide his or her score before the group moves on;
- start with the positive areas first (even if the participants' score on a section is "good," the facilitator should ask the group what was positive enough to rate a "good" versus a "poor");
- rotate the initiation of questions so that he or she does not start with the same participant every time;
- try to combine comments or suggestions;
- encourage and include all the participants to take part in the quality circle experience and not just to say they agree with someone else's comments;
- summarize the positive points and the suggestions for improvement;
- tally the scores; and
- report on the findings.

The proposal writer can listen to the comments and the scores but cannot rebut or respond to them. If the proposal writer disagrees with some of the comments, he or she can simply discount them later. The coach's role is to look at how the scores from the different groups compare and to discuss the overall comments. Again, the positive comments should be discussed before discussing the comments on the areas to improve.

When the facilitator is done, the group should provide feedback to him or her on how well he or she performed. As in the quality circle, the group should start with the most positive areas first and then tell the facilitator how he or she could improve his or her performance.

At the conclusion of the quality circle all copies of the proposal should be returned to the proposal writer.

Exhibit 16.4 is a sample of the handout I distribute in my quality circle training sessions and includes:

- rules of the game;
- a checklist for organizing and conducting a quality circle;
- how to select participants;
- the purpose of the activity;
- how to create the setting;

The Rules of the Game

To Play You Must Know:

- Who reads the proposal
- What their educational background is
- How they are trained
- What the scoring rubric/criteria is
- How the reviewers are selected
- Where the proposals are read
- How many proposal each reviewer reads
- How much time is spent on each proposal
- Whether there are primary reviewers who spend more time on the proposal
- How the scores are tabulated
- How the differences are discussed

Checklist for Organizing and Conducting a Quality Circle

_____ Selection of 4 or 5 reviewers/participants to assist in the mock review/quality circle exercise

_____ Invitation and transmittal of the instructions for the reviewers/participants

_____ Information on past grantees and results of pre proposal contact with grantor staff

_____ Transmit proposal and relevant information to participants with instructions/information on how to read the proposal and follow the actual scoring system that will be used, and the amount of time that the real reviewers will spend on the proposal.
(Note: If the proposal will be read in less than 30 minutes you may choose to actually read the proposal at the quality circle meeting so you can accurately model the time frame and conditions.)

_____ If the participants are to read the proposal in advance of the quality circle meeting, they should be instructed on what to bring to the meeting - such as the proposal and scores for each section, the positive areas highlighted, and the suggestions on the areas to be improved.

Selecting Participants

- Try to recruit at least two colleagues with content expertise
- Recruit at least one individual who has attended this training seminar
- Recruit an individual with a background/degree in communication, English, or a related area
- Recruit individuals who have prepared proposals

Exhibit 16.4   Using Quality Circles to Improve Proposals.

Purposes of this Activity

The purposes of this activity are to:

- receive the best possible feedback to improve your proposal and increase your score/rating
- involve more of your peers in using this activity to increase higher quality proposals and improve the image of your organization/institution with grantors and reviewers
- teach others the value of incorporating quality circles in their grant seeking

Creating the Setting

- Feed them and they will come
- Large enough room, proper temperature
- Select convenient time, but be creative and ask what will work for your volunteers
- Let them know you will reciprocate and volunteer for them

Roles/Sequence for Your Quality Circle Review

GROUP FACILITATOR – The group leader/facilitator is responsible for keeping the group on task, having the group focus on the proposal's positive aspects before moving on to the areas that need improvement, and reinforcing a constructive learning atmosphere. The facilitator may engage in reading and scoring the sections as well, but should reserve his/her comments and scores till last. The group leader may decide to facilitate discussion only if that is his/her desire.

The facilitator will request the scores for each section or part of the proposal before asking for the positive areas and areas to be improved. The facilitator is advised to rotate the request for comment to start each section among the participants, and to encourage everyone to participate. The facilitator will set a constructive tone and learning focus by asking each participant for his/her positive comments first, and will interrupt any participant who moves to the areas to be improved before each participant has presented his/her positive comments. After all positive comments have been presented the focus will turn to the areas that need to be improved in order to raise the score for each section.

PROPOSAL WRITER(S)/INITIATOR(S) – The creator(s) of the proposal under review may choose to either attend the quality circle meeting, or not to be present and just receive the results. If present, they should not be allowed to interrupt the process, defend the proposal, or provide any additional information (except in the beginning of the process). Before the quality circle starts the proposal initiator(s)/writer(s) may provide a short introduction including information learned through pre proposal contact or from successful grantees or past reviewers to help prepare the participants.

QUALITY CIRCLE PARTICIPANTS – The exercise participant is expected to adhere to the suggestions on reading time frames, developing helpful comments, and the scoring of each section. They are allowed to raise questions, but asking questions of the proposal writer(s)/initiator(s) should only be allowed when necessary to promote a realistic review.

Exhibit 16.4 *(continued)*

PROPOSAL REVIEW SEQUENCE – The proposal sequence to be followed should mirror that which the actual review will undergo. One exception is in the evaluation of the title and abstract/summary. It is suggested that the participants read, score, and discuss the impact that the title and abstract/summary had on their expectations of what the project was about, and the impression it gave them concerning the organization of the proposal.

Common Major Problems

- Mock reviewers using their own point of view to phrase their comments. (Begin with, "I think the reviewers would …")
- Starting with the things that need to be improved and not spending equal time commenting on the proposal's positive attributes. (Start with the positive areas and balance the time equally between the positive areas and the areas to be improved.)
- Not equating time spent on each area with the points or program emphasis allocated by the grantor research. (Review the scoring rubric and any other information you may have on the funding's sources proposal areas of priority.)
- Asking people to participate in your quality circle who have no training. (When possible, you should invite other colleagues who have been trained to participate in and/or facilitate quality circles.)

The Quality Circle Process

1. Instruct your participants to read the proposal in the same sequence as the actual reviewers. They may not be read in the order that are placed in the application.
2. Most reviewers start with the TITLE. Ask your participants to read the title and record what they think the proposal is about.
3. Review the application instructions relative to preparation of the summary/abstract. Ask you participants to read the summary or abstract and give it a score/rating. Discuss the positive points and the areas to improve.
4. Review the title and the notes relative to what they thought the project was concerned with, the application instructions, and what was presented in the abstract/summary. Provide a score and comments on how well these match and support one another.
5. After recording the scores, the positive points, and suggestions for improving the title and abstract/summary, move on to the next area.
6. Continue the process for each section of the proposal.
7. If the grantor's scoring rubric calls for overall scores or ratings, perform these at the end of the quality circle.
8. Thank the participants for their time and assistance. In many cases, they will even volunteer to review your changes.

Exhibit 16.4 (*continued*)

- quality circle roles and sequence;
- common, major problems; and
- an overview of the quality circle process.

My hope is that you find a great deal of gratification from showing your coachees how to use this great technique for improving their proposals. Once they have applied their quality circle suggestions for improvement to their proposals, they will be ready to submit them and you will be ready to help them in the process.

Chapter Seventeen

Role of the Coach in the Proposal Submission and Follow-Up Process

It is the responsibility of the grants coach to make sure that the work involved in proactive grant seeking results in their coachees' proposals being submitted on time or even better, a few days early. As a grants coach, you have probably had to deal with submittal rules in your previous grants experience. Even if you have this experience with universities and/or other nonprofit organizations, it is important to have a rudimentary knowledge of the process at the institution sponsoring your grants coaching program. I suggest you contact the office responsible for submission and let them know you have concern and respect for what they do. You may even invite someone from this office to provide the coachees with a brief overview of the institution's/organization's submittal process and its required forms.

Coachees do not need to know their institution's Data Universal Numbering System's number, its System for Award Management number, or its Employment Identification Number, but they should know that the institution handling their grant proposal takes care of all of this. Many aspiring grantees do not even know that they cannot submit a federal proposal themselves and that all federal proposals must be submitted through their institution's Authorized Organizational Representative (AOR). Educating the coachees on their institution's submittal process and the vast array of requirements related to the submittal of federal proposals will increase their appreciation for the staff that is responsible for handling these tasks.

A few coachees from one of the grants coaching programs I facilitated complained to me that they had completed all the proactive grant-seeking steps I suggested and got their proposals to their grants office two weeks prior to the deadline only to be informed that they were submitted late due to a computer malfunction and that the federal program agreed to allow the late submittal. When I looked into the problem, I discovered that it was the research office's protocol to prioritize proposals by deadline first. Therefore, proposals submitted two weeks early were put on the back burner so that the office could address the last-minute proposals that were likely to miss their strictly enforced deadlines if they were not given immediate attention.

Naturally, my coachees found this situation frustrating and surprising, and there was nothing I could do about it! The grant/research submittal administrator had always done it that way, and even after I spoke with her, she was not willing to change. So, as the coach, you should locate the responsible office and AOR, learn about the submittal process at the sponsoring institution, and share the information with your coachees.

It may be possible for you to arrange a one- or two-hour training session where the members from the Institutional Review Board (IRB) and the individuals responsible for human subjects' review present the protocol for obtaining the necessary clearances for their office. Try to arrange this training after you have initiated your program and have your coachees moving ahead on their grants quest. Too many institutions give presentations on the rules governing grants at new faculty orientations, only to overwhelm the novice grant seekers. Determine the sequence of knowledge for your program, make certain it coincides with your new grant seekers' needs, and helps them to progress positively in their coachee experience. Coachees do not need to be burdened with IRB and sign-off procedures before they even have a proposal idea and a potential grantor.

Grants coaching programs often do not provide follow-up contact with coachees. In most of the coaching programs I have facilitated, no support was provided after the coachees graduated from the program. However, I believe there are two coachee groups that could benefit from follow-up after completion of the program.

The first group consists of coachees who have submitted proposals and either have them still pending at the time of the program's completion or have had them denied. The institution has invested in these coachees and should recognize that they may need just a little follow-up to bring them beyond a proposal rejection. The coach can provide valuable assistance in recrafting a rejected proposal. The coachee can either reapply with the recrafted proposal or adapt the proposal to a new grantor.

Once when interviewing a new coachee I inquired about her past submittals and results. She had a rejected federal proposal she submitted two years before and reviewers' comments. It was her first attempt at a federal grant, and the reviewers' comments and scores were not that bad. None of the reviewers suggested she resubmit, but the proposal had areas of serious merit.

I coached her into contacting the program officer to discuss resubmittal or assistance in locating a more appropriate grants program. When she did so, the program officer wanted to know why she had not contacted her sooner. She remembered the proposal and was actually waiting to receive a resubmittal with improvements suggested by the reviewers. Eventually, my coachee's resubmittal was approved, but she lost two years' time.

That made me think about how many of my coachees did not reapply and how I could have assisted them with follow-up after the program was over. A quick review of submittals by grants coaching program graduates is all that would be necessary to see who should be recontacted for follow-up.

The second group that could benefit from follow-up consists of successful, awarded coachees. A short follow-up contact could validate:

- what the successful coachee found to be the most useful a year or two after achieving funding and completion;
- what problems the successful coachee encountered post-award and what could be done to make the post-award experience more positive; and
- how the successful coachee's experiences with funding will affect his/her future use of grant funding to reach his/her professional goals and objectives.

The follow-up you conduct with your grants coaching program graduates will help you improve your curriculum. You may decide to invite selected graduates from your past programs to make a short presentation to your current coachees to emphasize curricula points and validate the importance of persistence. A survey of past coachees may also demonstrate to your sponsoring institution that a small contract for selected follow-up could maximize the investment it has already made in the grants coaching program.

So, as you can see, follow-up is very important, and it is a subject you should discuss with your sponsoring institution/organization.

Chapter Eighteen

Guiding Coachees through the Foundation/Corporate and Private Proposal Development Process

While accessing the private grants marketplace can be very profitable, I start the focus of my grants coaching with federal grants because the federal government has approximately $500 billion in grant support while private grantors account for $50 to $60 billion. Also, when approaching private grantors, it is best for coachees to mention that they went to the federal government first and learned from that experience that their project/research did not meet the federal government's granting qualifications.

Private grant sources usually require that proposals be submitted through a 501(c)3 tax exempt entity. When working with institutions of higher education, this often means that your coachees' proposals must be submitted through a university foundation. The university's grants/research office will usually contact the university's foundation and alert them that they are handling a private proposal which will be submitted to the university's foundation for sign-off and transmission to the grantor.

The private grants marketplace can be very lucrative for inexperienced investigators as well as experienced investigators who are changing focus or breaking into new research areas. Therefore, the coach must dispel major misconceptions that coachees generally have about the private marketplace. If the coach does not deal with these misconceptions early on, they are bound to negatively affect how the coachees approach this marketplace.

At this place in the coachee's development of a successful approach to the private marketplace, I use a decades-old theory from psychology on how to understand how other people are likely to view the coachee and his or her proposal. Of course, this has to do with how the coachee views the private grants marketplace as well. Review chapter 3 of *The "How To" Grants* Manual and exhibit 3.1 on values-based grant seeking to increase your understanding of how your coachees' perceptions become their reality and influence their decision making.

My experiences have shown me that coachees generally have a myopic view of the grants world. Their tunnel vision leads them to focus on what they want and not on what grantors want and need. By explaining Festinger's Theory of Cognitive Dissonance as presented in *The "How To" Grants Manual* to your coaches, you can help them view the grants' world from the grantor's perspective. You will get them to begin to understand what grantors want to realize from each of their grants transactions and what the world looks like through their values glasses.

In the grants' world it is very important to write toward the reader's point of view. This is relatively easy to accomplish at the federal level since the reviewers are experts in the potential grantees' fields. However, this task becomes much more difficult in the private grants marketplace because those reviewing the proposals are not peers and their knowledge levels are often not known. Making the task of writing for the private grantor even more difficult is the fact that those reviewing the submitted proposals are often wealthy individuals with entirely different worldviews from their prospective grantees.

To help my coachees understand these differences I distribute lottery tickets in my classes and ask my coachees to imagine they have won the lottery. In order to keep their tickets, the coachees must promise to use their newfound wealth to fund the project/research they are proposing. Some of my coachees have said they would not fund their own project/research with their own money and that they only would do it with a grantor's money. Obviously, that's not a great attitude, but the exercise does help coachees think about how wealthy individuals might look at their proposals and their worthiness. Remind your coachees that the point of this exercise is to start thinking like the people with the money. (If you include the review of a short foundation or corporate proposal in your grants' seminar program, be sure to ask the coachees to view it from the perspective of a wealthy board member.)

One word of caution: Use discretion with this role-playing and lottery ticket distribution. Provide an option for those coachees who frown upon gambling. I once made the mistake of giving out lottery tickets at a religiously affiliated institution only to find out that many of my seminar participants were totally against any form of gambling. However, the dean of the college assured the participants it would be okay to gamble this one time if they promised to use their winnings to do their proposed grant projects and to give the balance to the church.

To dispel your coachees' misconceptions about the private marketplace, I recommend you administer the nonprofit marketplace quiz (exhibit 18.1) before your coachees approach this important marketplace. I can assure you that most of your coachees' answers to the questions will be wrong. Why? Because many of them will not agree with the correct answers and, as Festinger's theory states, when faced with information (facts) that we do not agree with, the filters through which we view the world allow us to ignore the truth.

So, as their coach, do not just give them the correct answers. If you do, they will nod their heads and promptly forget the facts. To emphasize the correct information, ask inductive questions and encourage group discussion. This might help your coachees put down their rose-colored values glasses and approach the private marketplace logically. Ask your coachees to make their best guesses on each of the quiz questions.

Question 1 asks approximately how many nonprofit organization were eligible to receive gifts and grants in 2015. The purpose of this question is to show your coachees that they will have a lot of competition. The correct answer is 1,521,052.

NON-PROFIT MARKETPLACE QUIZ

1. In the United States, approximately how many non-profit organizations - 501(c)(3s) – were eligible to receive gifts and grants in 2015?
   A.   50,239
   B.   511,485
   C.   1,521,052
   D.   853,428

2. What is the total amount of support granted to non-profit organizations from the federal government through their 1,000 plus grant programs?
   A. $100 billion
   B. $200 billion
   C. $300 billion
   D. $500 billion

3. What was the total amount of private and corporate money donated to non-profit organizations as tax deductible gifts in 2015?
   A. $ 10 billion
   B. $ 26 billion
   C. $133 billion
   D. $373 billion

4. The total amount of money donated to non-profit organizations comes from the following four basic sources. Indicate the percentage attributed to each source.
   Foundation Grants   _____ %
   Corporate Grants   _____ %
   Bequests   _____ %
   Individual Giving   _____ %

5. Approximately how many independent <u>grant</u> <u>making</u> foundations are there?
   A.   17,200
   B.   46,403
   C.   72,000
   D.   96,580

6. Approximately how many foundations occupy an office to conduct day-to-day business?
   A.   3,000   C.   10,000
   B.   5,000   D.   40,000

7. How many FT individuals are employed by foundations to help in their granting process?
   A.   4,000   C.   10,000
   B.   6,000   D.   40,000

Exhibit 18.1   Nonprofit Marketplace Quiz.

8.	What percent of a foundation's assets must be distributed in the form of grants each year?
	A. 2.0% B. 5.0% C. 7.5% D. 10.0%

9. The following areas represent the major recipients of foundation funding. Rank order from 1 through 10 with 1 receiving the greatest portion of funding and 10 the least.

Religion	_____	Public Society Benefit	_____
Arts & Culture	_____	Environment/Animals	_____
Health	_____	International Affairs	_____
Education	_____	Science & Technology	_____
Human Services	_____	Social Science	_____

10. Approximately how many U.S. companies are there?
    A. 500,000   B. 1,500,000   C. 12,000,000   D. 33,000,000

11. What percent of corporate pre-tax dollars are currently allowed to be taken as corporate deductions?
    A. 1.0%   B. 2.0%   C. 5.0%   D. 10.0%

12. The following areas represent the major recipients of corporate giving. Rank order from 1 through 9, with 1 being the greatest and 9 the least.

Culture/Arts	___	Community/Economic Development	___
Higher Education	___	Civic/Public Affairs	___
Environment	___	Disaster Relief	___
Health/Social Services	___	K-12 Education	___
		Other	___

13. Approximately how many corporate foundations are there in the United States?
    A. 1,250   B. 3,150   C. 5,000   D. 10,850

14. Which one of the following forms of corporate support for non-profit organizations experienced the greatest increase in 2013?
    A. Company Products   B. Cash   C. Securities   D. Loans

15. Which of the following examples most closely represents enlightened corporate self-interest?
    A. Computer Company X donates two interactive computer terminals to School District A to develop a model for home/school tutoring programs.
    B. Company X sets up a scholarship fund at its chief executive officer's college of choice.
    C. Company X joins a corporate 1% Club, and it contributes 1% of its net earnings before taxes (NEBT) to the local United Way.
    D. Company X requires that its employees be volunteers in all organizations applying for grants.

Exhibit 18.1   (continued)

Question 2 focuses on the total amount of federal support granted to nonprofit organizations. Your coachees will probably be shocked by the overwhelming amount of support provided by the federal government. The correct answer is $500 billion. When discussing this question, remind your coachees that many private grantors will want to know whether the grant seeker approached the federal marketplace first.

Question 3 asks about the total amount of private and corporate money donated to nonprofit organizations. The answer to this question will help your coachees understand the magnitude of the entire private marketplace. The correct answer is $373 billion.

Of the total $373 billion awarded in 2015, question 4 addresses the total amount donated by the four basic sources of funds—foundation grants (16 percent or $58.46 billion), corporate grants (5 percent or $18.45 billion), bequests (9 percent or 31.76 billion), and individual giving (71 percent or $264.58 billion). As the coach, you will be surprised that most of your coachees will think that 30 to 40 percent of private funding is derived from foundation grants—far more than the real 16 percent. This is because many of them think that all foundation grants are like the million dollar awards published in the *Chronicle of Philanthropy* and other journals.

They will also be shocked to find out that corporate support only accounts for 5 percent of the total. Help them to realize that their overestimates of corporate support come from corporate marketing and public relations. By discussing the correct answers to this question, your coachees will better understand the private marketplace and not make the mistake of requesting more private money than federal money.

Question 5 asks your coachees to estimate the number of independent grant-making foundations. Once they discover there are over ninety-six thousand they may feel a bit overwhelmed and rush to judgment about the amount of research that will be necessary to locate the right foundation for their projects/research. Calm their fears by letting them know that researching foundation databases are relatively easy and that only a chosen few prospective grantors will result from their searches. In my presentations, this is where I also provide my coachees with information on the different types of foundation. For more on this, see chapters 21 and 22 in *The "How To" Grants Manual*.

Questions 6 and 7 address the number of foundations with offices and staff. The answers to these questions will help your coachees realize that the private marketplace is markedly different from the federal marketplace. While federal grantors have offices and staff that can respond to coachees' preproposal contact inquiries, it is estimated that only three thousand grant-making foundations have offices and that less than ten thousand full-time individuals are employed by foundations. On the positive side, these space and staff restrictions are what leads foundations to request shorter proposals than their federal counterparts.

Question 8 on the percentage of assets a foundation must distribute in the form of grants each year will provide some encouragement to your coachees since all foundations, even those with no office or professional staff, are required to distribute 5 percent of their assets which accounts for billions of dollars.

Question 9 asks your coachees to rank order the areas representing the major recipients of foundation funding. The answers to this question will help your coachees to determine how much of the foundation marketplace relates to their areas of interest. They will also show your coachees how redefining their projects could increase their chances of attracting funding. The correct answers for 2015 contributions are religion, 3 percent; arts and culture, 13 percent; health, 13 percent; education, 20 percent; human services, 27 percent; public society benefit, 12 percent; environment/animals,

7 percent; international affairs, 2 percent; science and technology, 2 percent; and social science, 1 percent.

Question 10 asks how many companies there are in the United States. Estimates are that there are approximately thirty-three hundred thousand. While data are not easily obtained on the number that make grants, the available statistics make it seem that corporations have not reached their giving potential.

Question 11 asks what percentage of corporate pretax dollars are currently allowed to be taken as corporate deductions. The answer is 10 percent. When discussing this question with your coaches, point out that it is obvious from the answer that corporations do not succeed by giving away their profits. Also let them know that while the limit is 10 percent, the actual figure is not even close to that. History shows us that in 1985 corporations granted 2 percent of their net earnings before taxes (NEBT). By 2014 this figure had eroded to 0.7 percent.

Question 12 provides the coachees with data on what areas represent the major recipients of corporate giving. This information can be helpful to them when redefining their projects. The correct answers are culture/arts, 6 percent; higher education, 13 percent; environment, 5 percent; health/social services, 26 percent; community/economic development, 13 percent; civic/public affairs, 5 percent; disaster relief, 2 percent; K-12 education, 16 percent; and other, 16 percent.

Question 13 asks for an estimate of the number of corporate foundations in the United States. It is interesting that while there are an estimated 33 million corporations in the United States, there are only 3,150 corporate foundations. Even more interesting is the fact that these corporate foundations are responsible for only $5.43 billion of the $18.45 billion in total corporate grant support.

Question 14 focuses on the various vehicles that corporations use to support nonprofit organizations. In 2013 cash experienced the greatest increase and accounted for 83 percent of corporate support. The other 17 percent was derived from company products, securities, and loans.

What is not represented in these figures is donated equipment and products that are not taken as federal tax deductions. If your coachees' projects include significant expenditures on products, software, and/or equipment, it is possible that a corporation could benefit from donating or loaning them. Therefore, you should help your coachees access this "special" corporate marketplace. If a corporation can gain significant positioning value and/or increased sales from donating equipment, it might just do so. Since many university and community groups perform model projects that are designed to be disseminated and replicated by others, the potential for marketplace positioning and future sales may be very appealing to the corporation's marketing program.

If your coachee's project involves a creative or novel use of equipment, the manufacturer may be interested in supporting the project/research because it has the potential to add to the company's product development.

It has been my experience that companies often take the cost of donated products or equipment out of their sales or marketing budgets, thereby decreasing their profits. Not only does this transfer of property reduce the company's net earnings before it pays taxes, but it also does not have to be declared on the company's corporate foundation's IRS tax return. So, while cash is the largest form of support given by corporations to nonprofit organizations, your coachees should be made aware of the fact that there is potential for other forms of corporate support that are not reported as tax deductible donations.

Question 15 focuses on enlightened corporate self-interest and is included in the quiz to help coachees approach support from the corporate donor's point of view. Of the examples provided in the question, the computer company that donates two interactive computer terminals to a school district to develop a model for home/school tutoring program best represents enlightened corporate self-interest.

Essentially, your coachees should be made aware of the fact that corporate donors are always interested in what they get out of each transaction. The guiding philosophy for corporate philanthropy is quid pro quo.

Even a grant that does not benefit a company's bottom line may be awarded because it has the potential to benefit the company's workers or the community it is in and, hence, position the company as a socially responsible corporation.

As a coach, you can also use this question to initiate a discussion on corporate language. Once I had a corporate contributions officer attend one of my grants seminars. During the seminar I commented on the areas corporations generally give money to. On the afternoon break, the corporate contributions officer admonished me for using the word *give*. He reminded me that corporations never *give away* anything, including money. They *invest* in nonprofit organizations and expect a *return* on their investments. This corporate language conversation will help you reaffirm with your coachees the guiding principle of most companies' grants programs—enlightened corporate self-interest.

Chapter Nineteen

Integrating the Institution's/Organization's Grants Administration Staff into Your Grants Coaching Program

Irrespective of how effective your grants coaching is in helping your coachees prepare exceptional proposals, grants success depends on getting those proposals out of your organization and into the hands of the potential grantors. As a former research administrator I dedicated years to improving the efficiency of grants/research administrative systems. It is critically important that each proposal leaving your sponsoring institution/organization is a credit to its image and demonstrates respect for the grantor's stated rules and regulations.

Few proposal development staff or grant writing faculty/researchers understand the myriad of rules and regulations that proposals must meet to gain institutional approval. The term academic freedom is interpreted by many faculty and researchers to mean that they, the experts, should be allowed to submit anything they deem appropriate to any grantor. Your sponsoring institution's/organization's grants administrator is not the content expert that the researcher/proposal developer is. However, the administrator knows the grants submission process and the assurances, rules, and regulations that the grantee is responsible for following.

Your grants coaching program provides you with an opportunity to deal proactively with your sponsoring institution's/organization's grants/research administration by offering appropriate seminar and proposal development learning activities. This does not mean that you abrogate your role and allow the grants/research administrator free reign over your seminar/learning experience. However, it does make sense to involve him/her early in your program. I suggest you invite him/her to make a presentation at your first seminar. Advise him/her of the topics you would like to have touched upon and the time frame for the presentation.

There is a scope and sequence to what your coachee/proposal developer needs to know about the role of grants/research administration and when he/she should be introduced to this knowledge. I have witnessed well-intended but overly detailed presentations that could convince most proposal writers to stop their grant seeking immediately.

Approach the inclusion of this information by reminding the grants/research administrator that his/her presentation to your coachees/grant seekers is to be limited to an *introduction* to the role and purpose of grants/research administration. Your coachees do not need to be experts on the Code of Federal Regulations or the Office of Management and Budget (OMB) circulars because the grants/research administrator is the one that knows the rules and will help them avoid problems in this area.

There are two entirely different administrative offices that you should include in your programs—one that governs federal and state proposals and one that governs foundation and corporate proposals. Each of these offices represent portals for the proposal submission process, and each one must provide permission to apply to a grantor. To ensure that your coachees have a general knowledge of the two systems, I suggest you invite the appropriate administrator from each to attend your seminar, present a brief description of his/her office, and describe what assistance it provides to grant seekers. Since the federal government has ten times more grants funds than foundations and corporation, I suggest presenting the government seminar before presenting the foundation and corporate grants seminar.

Your invitation should include the background of the grants coaching program, your curriculum and agenda for each of the appropriate seminars, and the time frame in which you would like the grants/research administrator to make his/her presentation. This chapter provides you with worksheets that suggest what you may want to include in your communication. The purpose of your invitation is to familiarize the administrator with your text, curriculum, and specific topics that integrate well with the coachees' learning experience.

It is important to tell the administrator that this early-on input is meant to be proactive, that it may be months before your coachees are actually at the submittal stage, and that his/her presentation is meant as an introduction. There will be time for interaction later that will be more appropriate in terms of proposal development. You can also mention to the administrator that it would be useful to schedule follow-up sessions on assistance with database searching, budgeting, and/or submission at dates that are appropriate to the grants processes that the coachees are learning.

As more universities adopt computer programs for pre- and post-grants activities, the appropriate administrators may present shorter mini-sessions throughout your grants coaching program to ensure compliance and compatibility of your curriculum to the institution's/organization's policies.

The goal of your interaction with the two grants administrative systems and portals for submission that your coachees encounter is the same. You want your coachees to produce grant-winning proposals that have the support and approval of their institution. However, most colleges, universities, and large nonprofit organizations distinguish between government grant proposals (federal, state, and local) and private grant proposals (foundation and corporate). Therefore, it is important to examine each separately.

1. *Government Proposals (Federal, State, and Local Publicly Funded Grants and Contracts)*

Colleges and universities have traditionally treated government grant funding differently from private funding. Offices in charge of government grants are often referred to as grants and research offices or offices of sponsored programs and research. These offices are responsible for assuring that all proposals emanating from its institution have followed the institution's regulations as well as the government agency's requirements.

Your coachees need to act early to get the required clearances related to the use of human subjects, animals, hazardous materials, and so on. However, at the beginning of your program they just need to know the appropriate individuals and offices to contact when the time comes. Ask your institution's grants administrator to brief your coachees on the process and how they can receive help submitting the appropriate forms, and so on.

It is important that your coachees know that their expenditures and budgets must follow a myriad of federal rules and regulations detailed in the OMB's circulars, federal assurances, and Institutional Review Board guidelines. The object is to inform the coachees without intimidating them. Work with the grants/research administrator to provide only as much information as the coachee needs to know now.

The administrator's presentation at your seminar should culminate with an explanation of the institution's submittal process. Many prospective grantees do not know that they cannot directly submit a proposal to a government program. They need to know who has been designated as their institution's Authorized Organizational Representative. This person (or these people) is the only one who can submit and meet the grant program deadline.

Have the administrator include information on how much internal time the submittal process requires to ensure that proposal deadlines are met. Since your grant seekers will be coached on the use of proactive techniques, they will want to get their proposals in early and will need to know if their institution's grants office handles proposals on a first-come, first-served basis or by deadline dates. Unfortunately, the deadline date basis rewards the last-minute grant seeker at the expense of the proactive early bird.

Some institutions subscribe to proposal review systems that can only be accessed if proposals are received a prescribed number of days before the actual deadline. In addition, they may have a "red team" or other review system they use to improve proposals before submittal. If this is the case, your coachees should take advantage of everything their institution makes available to them.

Colleges and universities are moving toward paperless submittal procedures where even the sign-off process is computerized. Make sure your coachees know the system so they can be sure their proposals will be sent to the government granting agency in the correct format and on time. Exhibit 19.1 outlines the steps you will need to take to include the sponsoring institution's government grants administrator in your grants coaching program.

> ____ Send e-mail introducing your grants coaching program
> ____ Provide invitation to present at your government grants seminar
> ____ Outline areas you would like them to address, such as:
> - assistance in searching for government grants opportunities,
> - data base training on opportunities available through *Grants.gov, Pivot, SPIN, FedBizOpps, GrantSelect, GrantSearch*, etc.
> - assistance with meeting requirements related to internal review boards (IRBs) and/or the use of human subjects, animals, hazardous materials, etc.,
> - rules governing the sign-off and submittal processes,
> - identifying the authorized organization representative (AOR),
> - assistance with budget development, and
> - the process for creating sub-contracts and consortia agreements.

Exhibit 19.1 Worksheet on How to Include Administrators Key to Government Proposal Preparation and Submittal.

2. *Private Proposals (Foundation, Corporate, and Other Nongovernment Grants)*

Most colleges and universities have a separate system for handling foundation, corporate, and other nongovernment grant proposals. The separation of private funding from government funding is done to control access to private grantors. In most higher-education institutions, foundations and corporations are viewed as proprietary by the institution's development office.

Your coachees must know the protocol for getting permission to approach and submit proposals to foundations and corporations before they invest their time in proposal preparation. They also need to know that the reason for preapproval is to avoid sending multiple or conflicting proposals to the same private grantor. Many foundations and corporations limit the number of proposals submitted by one institution; therefore, your coachees must be made aware of the importance of having their proposals preapproved and preprioritized by their institution.

The best method to get this information to your coachees is to have the appropriate administrator make a presentation at your foundation and corporate grants seminar. Exhibit 19.2 outlines the steps you will need to take to include the sponsoring institution's private grants administrator, often known as the development director, in your grants coaching program, and outlines what you would like the administrator to cover in the time frame you set aside for his/her presentation.

Not *all* colleges and universities separate the private grants marketplace from the public grants marketplace. In fact, my job description at the University of Rochester School of Medicine, Department of Pediatrics, included responsibility for government and private grants. Therefore, it is important that you recognize that each institution has its own way of dividing grant funding sources and that you will need to research your sponsoring institution's method and contact the appropriate administrators that govern the portals for proposal development and submission.

> _____ Send e-mail introducing your grants coaching program
> _____ Provide invitation to present at your foundation & corporate grants seminar
> _____ Outline areas you would like them to address, such as:
> - assistance in understanding the restrictions on contacting potential private grantors (if there are any) and the pre-approval requirements that must be met before contact is made
> - other rules, restrictions and the processes that must be followed when seeking private funding
> - assistance using the institution's/organization's private grantor searching data bases like the *Foundation Directory Online, NOZA, GrantSelect,* etc.
> - assistance with coordinating joint approval for assurances with the institution's/organization's government grants administrator(s)
> - identifying the authorized organizational representative (AOR) for dealing with foundations and corporations
> (Often the college or university's development office will act in this capacity)
> - providing guidance with the submission of foundation and corporate grant proposals including how to obtain the signature of the highest ranking administrator from the appropriate office like institutional advancement or development

Exhibit 19.2 Worksheet on How to Include Administrators Key to Private Proposal Preparation and Submittal.

Several areas of private grants administration, like human subjects and IRB approval, may require coordination with the sponsoring institution's office for the administration of government grant proposals. Development offices that deal with foundation and corporate grants usually do not have the administrative structure necessary to ensure the institution's exposure against injury in proposals that require the use of human subjects or hazardous materials. In fact, these and the other assurances provided to government-funded proposals may not be considered at all in the private grants sign-off process. It is your job to protect your coachees from legal and ethical problems that could arise. Therefore, you should check with the institution's appropriate administrators to learn how they handle these important issues.

Whether your coachees will be working with their institution's public and/or private grants administrator, it is best to have a face-to-face discussion with the appropriate administrator to explain how you would like him/her to interact with your coachees. Exhibits 19.1 and 19.2 provide the basis for these discussions.

In my consulting work I am not always available to meet face to face with the sponsoring institution's grants administrators. In these cases, I use e-mail and phone contact to discuss the areas I would like them to include in their presentations and the time frames I would like them to abide by during my seminars. Exhibits 19.3 and 19.4 are sample e-mails that can be adapted to your situation and used for this purpose.

From: <grants coach>
To: <institution's/organization's government grants administrator>
Subject: Invitation to Present at Government Grants Seminar

Dear [Government Grants Administrator]:

I have been charged with developing and conducting a grants coaching program at [institution/organization]. The goal of this educational experience is to increase the knowledge and experience of your grant seekers and to increase the external resources that will help to support your institution's/organization's mission. The program seeks to prepare the participants to develop and submit, successful government, foundation, and corporate proposals.

The program consists of [number] educational seminars and [number of hours] of individual consulting over [period of time]. One of the seminars is on how to find and win government grants. I will be presenting this seminar on [date] at [place] from [time] to [time] to introduce the program participants to the government grants marketplace.

It would be beneficial to the participants to be introduced to your office and staff, to be briefed on the procedures they must follow at the later stages of their proposal development, and to learn about the services your office provides such as grants data base searches, development and maintenance of research/grants profiles, etc. I feel your office's input is critical to insuring that my program participants conduct their proposal preparation and submission within your institution's/organization's guidelines.

I invite you to have lunch with the seminar group on [date] at [time] at [place]. It would be great if you could provide a thirty to forty-minute overview of your office following our lunch. I would be happy to share my seminar agenda and curriculum with you and a copy of the seminar text so that you can familiarize yourself with the contents the participants will be exposed to prior to your talk.

I am available to discuss any of the areas relating to this request with you. I look forward to meeting you and to working with you collaboratively to demonstrate a smooth and accountable government grant proposal process to my grants coaching program participants.

Name
Title
Organization
Address
Phone Number

Exhibit 19.3 Sample E-mail Inviting Government Grants Administrator to Take Part in Your Seminar.

From: <grants coach>
To: <institution's/organization's private grants administrator>
Subject: Invitation to Present at Foundation & Corporate Grants Seminar

Dear [Private Grants Administrator]:

I have been charged with developing and conducting a grants coaching program at [institution/organization]. The goal of this educational experience is to increase the knowledge and experience of your grant seekers and to increase the external resources that will help to support your institution's/organization's mission. The program seeks to prepare the participants to develop and submit, successful government, foundation, and corporate proposals.

The program consists of [number] educational seminars and [number of hours] of individual consulting over [period of time]. One of the seminars is on how to find and win foundation and corporate grants. I will be presenting this seminar on [date] at [place] from [time] to [time] to introduce the program participants to the private grants marketplace. Later on in the year through my continued instruction, the program participants will be ready to go after the 16% of foundation grants available for research, the 1.3% available for curriculum development, the 43.9% for program/project support and will be advised to avoid capital campaigns, one of the areas normally reserved for development.

It would be beneficial to the participants to be introduced to your office and staff, to be briefed on the procedures they must follow to access non-governmental grant resources and the protocols they must adhere to before approaching private grantors, and to learn about the services your office may provide such as grants data bases searches. They also need to know how the process of sign-off is handled when the grantor is asking for the institution's/organization's 501 © 3 designation and the signature of that entity to guarantee institutional commitment.

I invite you to have lunch with the seminar group on [date] at [time] at [place]. It would be great if you could provide a thirty to forty-minute overview of your office following our lunch. I would be happy to share my seminar agenda and curriculum with you and a copy of the seminar text so that you can familiarize yourself with the contents the participants will be exposed to prior to your talk.

I am aware of how important coordination is to approaching private grantors in an organized and credible manner and feel that your office's input is critical to insuring that my program participants conduct their foundation and corporate proposal preparation and submission within your institution's/organization's guidelines.

I am available to discuss any of the areas relating to this request with you. I look forward to meeting you and to working with you collaboratively to demonstrate a smooth and accountable private grant proposal process to my grants coaching program participants.

Name
Title
Organization
Address
Phone Number

Exhibit 19.4 Sample E-mail Inviting Private Grants Administrator (Development Director) to Take Part in Your Seminar.

Chapter Twenty

Evaluating and Improving Your Grants Coaching Program

Review chapters 1, 4, and 8 of this book and identify the objectives that were established as markers of success for your grants coaching program. Then review the measurement indicators that were originally discussed. Most grants/research administrators prefer to use easily measurable statistical indicators like an increase in the success rate of submitted proposals or an increase of funding from external grantors.

While it is important to compare the cost of a program with its return in grants dollars, grants coaching programs should also be evaluated on whether they fostered their institution's/organization's values and furthered its mission. For example, indicators like dollars generated from the program or indirect costs recaptured do not take into consideration smaller grants that do not bring in big bucks or pay indirect costs but do significantly contribute to curriculum and program enhancement. While it can be contended that smaller grants cost the institution/organization time and effort that could be spent on larger grants that generate indirect costs, this argument ignores the many attributes that smaller grants create.

The benefits resulting from any grants/research effort, including a grants coaching program, should be documented. But this documentation must include whether the outcomes of the effort or program support the mission of the institution/organization. For instance, in my work with a college of arts and sciences, the dean values smaller, humanities grants because one of his priorities is to strike a balance between the humanities discipline and scientific research.

There is no doubt that your client needs to evaluate and justify its investment in your grants coaching program. But as it does, it must look at the specific groups involved in your program and the changes that occurred within these groups as a result of your program.

Several of my clients have asked for specific data on how coachees fare compare to noncoachees with respect to past grant submittals and awards with specific funding agencies, such as the National Institutes of Health, the National Science Foundation, the National Endowment for the Humanities, the US Department of Education, the National Endowment for the Arts, and others.

I have not been able to satisfy their requests because we did not set up pre- and postevaluations by agency or by type of funding vehicle (i.e., R01, R15, and so on). However, when compared to past submissions by all researchers in a college, my coachees have experienced over 50 percent success. One other interesting variable that could be analyzed is the success rate of first-time proposal submittal by coachees compared to the success rate of other faculty, first-time submittals.

While it is understandable that those paying for the grants coaching program are looking for measurements that relate to cost effectiveness and accountability for expenditures, as the coach you are concerned with evaluating the success of your curriculum and the specific strategies you encourage your coachees to practice. I encourage you to elicit feedback on your curriculum and your presented strategies throughout your training seminars and face-to-face coaching sessions.

Exhibit 20.1 is an example of a generic evaluation form that can be used after each of your seminars. It is designed to elicit feedback on the seminar's curriculum and what the seminar participants, or coachees, think should be added, presented in greater detail, and/or eliminated in future presentations. One of the questions on the evaluation is whether the participant would recommend the seminar to a colleague. The responses to this question can be quite enlightening!

Exhibit 20.2 lists the major components of a proactive, grant-winning approach. As your coachees complete the program, ask them to review this list and check those strategies or actions they accomplished. Then have them rate how useful they found each of them.

It is important to provide feedback to the office responsible for your grants coaching program throughout its implementation, and not just at its conclusion. However, it should be pointed out that your coachees' incorporation of winning grants strategies take place over a time frame that is outlined in the program's announcement/application.

For example, I received an e-mail from one of my former coachees who had completed the program three years ago. He received a small grant for data collection. He collected his data over two years, had two journal articles published on his findings, and, as a result of his work, received the seminal grant award in this field. He believes what he learned the years before in the grants coaching program ultimately led to his success. Hence, completion of proactive strategies, submittal, and proposal award should all be considered part of the time frame when evaluating your grants coaching program.

One very pleasing component of my grants coaching programs is a ceremony or graduation that recognizes those who have completed the program. (Exhibit 4.9 in chapter 4 is a sample invitation to this graduation and exhibit 4.10 is a sample certificate of completion.) This occasion provides the opportunity to reference the program's and the coachees' accomplishments and I am always moved hearing about the successes.

Your Name (optional): _____
Seminar Title: _____ Date of Seminar _____

Please rate the 5 areas below using the following scale:
4 = Excellent, 3 = Good, 2 = Poor, 1 = Very Poor

Overall the seminar was	4	3	2	1
The instructor's presentation was	4	3	2	1
In terms of your needs, the seminar focus was	4	3	2	1
The written materials were	4	3	2	1
The class discussions were	4	3	2	1

Please rate the area below using the following scale:
4 = Just Right, 3 = Okay, 2 = Too Fast, 1 = Too Slow

The pace of the seminar was	4	3	2	1

What you liked most about the seminar:

Changes you feel would improve the seminar:

Would you recommend this seminar to others? _____ Yes _____ No

Exhibit 20.1 Sample Seminar Evaluation Form.

Put a check next to the proactive grant seeking strategies you have accomplished. Then rate the usefulness of the strategy with 1 being poor, 2 being fair, 3 being good, 4 being very good, and 5 being superior.

	Strategy	1	2	3	4	5
_____	Define the problem	1	2	3	4	5
_____	Brainstorm interventions	1	2	3	4	5
_____	Research grantors	1	2	3	4	5
_____	Develop advisory group and gather endorsements	1	2	3	4	5
_____	Obtain list of grantees	1	2	3	4	5
_____	Contact grantee(s) for copy of proposal	1	2	3	4	5
_____	Make pre-proposal contact	1	2	3	4	5
_____	Obtain reviewer information	1	2	3	4	5
_____	Conduct literature search	1	2	3	4	5
_____	Refine intervention, management plan, and evaluation design	1	2	3	4	5
_____	Develop a project plan/spreadsheet	1	2	3	4	5
_____	Develop a budget	1	2	3	4	5
_____	Conduct a quality circle on proposal draft	1	2	3	4	5
_____	Incorporate suggestions for improvement and submit	1	2	3	4	5
_____	Celebrate and thank grantors and advisors	1	2	3	4	5

Exhibit 20.2 Winning Grant-Seeking Strategy Checklist.

I can only hope that your grants coaching experiences are as gratifying as mine have been, and that this book leads you as a grants coach or you as an administrator of the sponsoring institution/organization on this very rewarding journey.

Index

Association for Coaching, 2
Authorized Organizational Representative (AOR), 113, 127

career grants/research plans, 63–70
Catalog of Federal Domestic Assistance, 81
certificate of completion, 29
Change Anything: The New Science of Personal Success (Patterson et al.), 54
coach. *See* grants coach
Coachee's Evaluation/Feedback Form, 62
Corporate Redefinition Worksheet, 82
Cost–Benefit Analysis Worksheet, 74, 75
Creative Research Activities Development and Enrichment (CRADLE) initiative, 18, 21, 23–24

educational components, 33–37
e-mail, 89, 130, 131

Federal Business Opportunities (FedBizOpps), 81
Federal Grants Research Form, 86
federal program officer:
    funding source staff profile, 96;
    preproposal contact with, 93–94;
    public funding source contact summary sheet, 96;
    questions for, 95;
    tailoring worksheet, 97
federal proposal development process, 99–101;
    uniqueness worksheet, 100

government proposals, 126–27, 128
graduation luncheon, sample invitation to, 28
Grants Acquisition Program, 30
grants administration staff, 125–31
grants coach:
    as change agent, 59–60;
    developing advocacy plans, consortia, and teams, 73–77;
    developing and maintaining research/grants profiles, 79–83;
    developing career grants/research plans, 63–70;
    evaluating and improving effectiveness of, 60–62;
    and focusing on the problem, 71–72;
    and foundation/corporate and private proposal development process, 117–23;
    goal of, 54;
    as mentor, 57–58;
    and proposal submission/follow-up process, 113–15;
    as reflective listener, 55–56;
    role of, 53–62, 103–11;
    as teacher/educator, 54–55
grants coaching program:
    benefit of, 8;
    college or university, 14;
    concept of, 2, 7;
    cost effectiveness of, 39–45;
    evaluating and improving, 133–36;
    goals of, 7–8;
    participants/target population, 13–15;

requirements/educational components, 18;
research development program, 29, 30;
structure of, 49–51
Grants Coaching Program Agreement, 27
grants coaching program outline:
  Creative Research Activities Development and Enrichment, 23–24;
  Grants Acquisition Program, 30;
  Public Relations/Marketing Piece, 21;
  Research Development Award Program, 19–20
grants consulting, 2
grants mentorship, 3–4
grants program application, 25
grants training, 2

The "How To" Grants Manual (Bauer), 9, 10, 33, 34–35, 44, 49, 55, 63, 67, 73, 76, 79, 81, 82, 85, 89, 93, 94, 99, 100–101, 103, 104, 117

Institutional Review Board (IRB), 114
International Coach Federation, 2

Marquette University, 24
McLean, James E., 15, 31
McNamara, Carter, 1–2

net earnings before taxes (NEBT), 122
Nonprofit Marketplace Quiz, 119–20

The Odyssey (Homer), 57

personal grants plan, 63–70
private proposals, 128–29
proactive grant seeking, 9–11

Program and Past Recipient Analysis Worksheet, 88
Pruitt, Samory T., 31

Redefinition/Key Search Terms Worksheet, 80
The Research-Productive Department (Bland et al.), 57
Rodgers, Carl, 55

"self-learning and improvement contract" concept, 3
seminar evaluation form, 135
seminar outline:
  foundation and corporate grants, 35;
  government grants, 34;
  improving grant proposals through quality circles, 37;
  keys to increasing collaboration and effective team building, 36
sign-up sheets, 26
Small Business Innovation Research, 1

tailoring worksheet, 90, 97
Theory of Cognitive Dissonance, 117

University of Alabama, 10, 18, 22, 24, 28, 29, 30, 31, 43
University of North Carolina Greensboro (UNCG), 24, 29, 58

video-recorded session, 60, 61

Wake Forest University (WFU), 18, 21, 25
Western Michigan University (WMU), 3–4
Winning Grants (Bauer), 10
Winning Grant-Seeking Strategy Checklist, 136

About the Author

David G. Bauer has authored ten books on grant seeking and fundraising over his forty-five-year career that included securing grants for school districts, universities, and nonprofit organizations while teaching over 45,000 participants in his seminars. Bauer has served as a national trainer for nonprofits, a foundation director, and a research director. In addition, he has directed several very successful grants coaching programs based on the proactive step-by-step system outlined in his *"How To" Grants Manual*.

www.ingramcontent.com/pod-product-compliance
Lightning Source LLC
Chambersburg PA
CBHW080939300426
44115CB00017B/2885